Road Trip!

A Guide to Absolutely the Best West Coast Drives, Ever

by
Steve McCarthy

**Tempting Lord Lucas, the Prince of Darkness, Mike Andrews
slogs through a water crossing on the Iron Bottom
photo by the author**

©2010 by Stephen McCarthy

mccARThy Vehicular & Architectural Portraits, Monrovia, CA www.mccarthypix.com

First Edition
ISBN 1449982808

1

Dedication

All of this would never have been as much fun without my co-driver-for-life, Marianne. She is the best of sports. Freezing, broiling, soaking, and holding it in when there just isn't a place to stop. Not many women would put up with this with her enthusiasm and good humor for these thirty years plus. *Gra mo chroi mo Mari*!

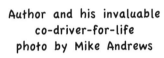

Author and his invaluable
co-driver-for-life
photo by Mike Andrews

Acknowledgments and Thanks

I'd like to first thank the Academy...oops, wrong speech! Lessee here...First and foremost is my family. My wife, Marianne, the girls-Brianna, Meaghan, and Caitlin have all endured hours in various cars and vans and not killed each other. In fact, since we started them early on Road Trippin', a long drive just to take a drive has become a family tradition. I also have to acknowledge Brianna for her editing. This was a huge job and beyond the brief for a dutiful daughter. Next, Bill Morgan and Bruce Jones, my two oldest friends and partners in crime. We met more years ago than any of us want to remember, driving buses for Embree's in Pasadena, fine tuning our Road Trippin' skills. Then there are Chuck Forward and Tina VanCurren of Autobooks in Burbank, CA. They gave me the opportunity to write my column in the *Automotive Calendar of Events,* and get this whole project started. I want to also thank Mike Andrews, Brianna McCarthy, and Marianne McCarthy for allowing me to use some of their photos, taken on a number of these trips. I want to thank Bill Morgan for revising my cover. He did a brilliant job. In addition, all the folks at Car Night for lots of ideas, writers such as Jean Shepard, Ciaran Carson, Henry Manny, Ted West, and Brock Yates for helping me find my own writing style, and a couple of guys named Daimler and Benz for inventing the infernal contraption we so love to drive and John Loudon McAdam, the guy who thought paving roads with his new gooey tar-like stuff would be a good idea.

Road Trippin'
Table of Contents

WHat iS a Road Trip...ANyWay?

A question of almost Talmudic proportions. Well then, let's talk Road Trips. Not the "Load-the-Kids-in-the-Mini-Van-Turn-on-the-DVD-and-Rush-to-Some-Far-Off-Theme-Park-Eating-Fast-Food-All-the-Way-on-the-Interstate-with-the-Cruise-Control-On-and-Yakking-on-Cell-Phone-Road-Trips;" trips that sadly confirm John Steinbeck's prediction: "soon, we will be able to drive coast to coast and never see anything." No, *real* Road Trips. Road Trips on back roads. Road Trips eating at Mom and Pop diners. Road Trips of odd souvenir stands and picnic lunches. Road Trips of spectacular scenery where the journey itself is the reward, and to top it off, you have to do it in a Real Car.

Since you are reading this book, I'm guessing you have some form of Real Car (or Bike), not an SUV with climate control, or at least, you want one. In my case, its a 1960 Triumph TR3 with racing windscreens, no top, loud exhaust, stiff suspension, and at times in the past, questionable reliability. Your vehicle may differ. Oh Yeah, let's make the Road Trip a LONG one. At least a couple of hundred miles in a day. Now *that's* what Road Trips are about! That's what this book is about, A Guide to Real Road Trips: route instructions to take you along some great roads, good places to eat, odd and unusual places to stop, everything a great Road Trip needs.

The Office
Next Page: Springtime on the coast brings out the flowers!
both photos by the author

Now don't think I'm leaving out you guys on motorcycles. Of all the gearheads out there, you are the ones that get the most out of your rides. Hitting the road is what you guys do. My background is in cars, so I tend to think and write that way. Believe me though, I admire you guys. You get colder and wetter than we do in my TR3! So don't get your knickers in a knot, I'm not leaving you out. Hell, you put *all* of us to shame when it comes to Road Trips, so this book is definitely for you too!

But first, can we talk? Seriously, I don't get some of you Hot Rod Guys. Now I have to tell you, my experiences as a Car Guy have been mostly shaped by sports cars. I have the aforementioned TR3, known as the Blue Meanie and in addition, I used to be a Turn Marshall for the SCCA, working such races as the Long Beach Grand Prix, endurance races at the old Riverside Raceway, and other assorted sporty car road races. I even worked at NASCAR races. Add to that the fact that I also worked for the late, lamented BAP/Geon selling

4

foreign car parts and you get the picture. Don't get me wrong, I'm not some purist snob. I *really* like Hot Rods and motorcycles. I'd like to build a hot rod myself one day. So don't think I'm trying to insult anyone. I just don't understand a part of what I've seen as the Hot Rod Mentality. Too often, the modern Hot Rodder's idea of a "Cruise" is to get the rod out of the garage, go someplace close, and *park*, then stand around and tell stories and

ogle each other's cars. Now, I've done this, and it can be fun, but, its a *car*. Drive the darn thing! Maybe it has to do with the fundamental difference in the kind of racing that attracts us. Hot Rodders come from

drag racing. Sit in line waiting to run, scope the other guys' cars, up to the line, green light, BOOM...pure acceleration and adrenaline for a few seconds and back in line, and stand around some more. Sports Car Guys come from a *whole* different idea of racing. The Le Mans 24 hour race, the Miglia Mille (a thousand miles of Italian back roads), the Targa Florio, the Carrera Pan-America. Races that are measured in hours rather than seconds. As a result, it seems Sports Car Guys are more about driving the cars than looking at them. Now this just makes Sports Car Guys and Hot Rod Guys *different*, not *better* than the other, and there are just as many Sports Car Trailer Queens as Hot Rod Trailer Queens. It does seem though, that too many Hot Rod Guys are missing a helluva good time by not getting out on the open road and *driving* their cars!

So clearly, we're talking about using cars for their intended purpose. Driving. We are also talking about nostalgia. A desire to turn back the clock to the era of our youths, or to an era we wish we had experienced. Remember that nostalgia isn't what it used to be! Those backroads that used to be main roads are still fraught with danger. Probably more so now than back then, because there's nobody else out there. At least when Route 66 was *the* highway, there was plenty of traffic and the probability of help. Today, these roads are far more deserted. Help (either mechanical or medical- we're all beyond the psychological) isn't a sure thing. And don't think the ubiquitous cell phone is an instant life line. A lot of the places this book takes you are out of touch with many service providers. Many of these roads aren't maintained all that well anymore, assuming they were ever maintained. So, keep your wits about you. Be prepared. But above all, have fun. These roads, and the surrounding scenery, are indeed magnificent and worth every gallon of fuel, every extra hour of drive time, every bump, every pothole, every possible frustration.

Preparation and Safety

Now before we talk about the Road Trip, let's talk a bit of preparation and safety. It seems silly to have to say this, but make sure your pride-and-joy is up to it. Treat Road Trip Preparation like Race Car Preparation. We are so used to modern cars that always seem to work, that we sometimes forget that taking your Auld Crate out for a serious drive needs a different approach. Most of us are probably better about maintenance for our old cars than our new cars, but that doesn't mean you don't make sure everything is just right before the trip. Carry tools and some basic parts. You can't just roll into a garage or parts store in East Overshoe, New Mexico and find stuff for your 1937 Pizwitz Mk.3! You're a Car Guy, you should know what to take along, but here's a basic list:

1. Set of spark plugs
2. Points, condenser (or a spare electronic module), distributor cap, rotor, plug wires
3. Fan belt
4. A couple of feet of gas line and clamps
5. Radiator hoses and clamps
6. Oil
7. At least a container for water, if not water.
8. Check that the jack and lug wrench are still in the car and work
9. Check that the spare tire has air
10. Spare tire in a can
11. Radiator stop leak
12. Rags
13. Drop cloth so when you're lying under the car in the mud, you don't get too sloppy. It can also double as a rain awning.
14. Electrical tape, wire, and various connectors
15. A few of the most common nuts and bolts
16. Tools to install or work on all of the above.
17. Cash. Some places still don't take plastic and ATMs, aren't universal.
18. And naturally, Racer's Tape!

In addition, bring things that will make the Road Trip more comfortable. If you have an open car, bring a jacket. In fact, bring a jacket anyway, you never know! The cold can surprise you, even in the summer. Bring some snacks. Various types of trail mix are good, cheap, and travel well. Beef jerky or a chub of salami and some cheese and good bread are always tasty. A small ice chest with some drinks (save the beer or wine for the evening, *after* the driving is done, *right?*) is always good plus, the water can help cool an overheating engine. If you have room, add a couple of small folding chairs or a blanket, especially if you plan on a picnic. If you can get an older copy of the *Thomas Bros. California Map Book*, great. At least have some AAA maps of the area in question. There is a new series of map books available from Autobooks in Burbank by Benchmark Maps called *Road and Recreation Atlases*. They're listed by state and provide good detailed information. They

6

are a bit large and aren't spiral bound, so you can't fold them back. Great for planning but a bit hard to use on the fly. I'm not a fan of GPS. Too many times they give the wrong info and have no idea where the odd back roads are. If you have one you trust, great, but bring a map anyway. I'm sure there are other things you can think of that are peculiar to your needs. Plan to be as self sufficient as you can, it makes life *so* much easier.

Then there is road safety. Yeah. Back roads are not race tracks. There are no safety crews with fire bottles out there to save you. There is cross traffic and on coming traffic, and animals, and stuff out there that can come as a *big* surprise and ruin your whole day. Stay comfortably within your and your car's limits. Also, stay within your *passenger's* limits! A White-Knuckled-Ashen-Faced-Floor-Board-Stomping-About-To-Puke-Seat-Mate really is no fun at all! *Especially* if it's your spouse! Agree on a polite signal (my wife pats me on the leg) that says, "Please Back Off For a Bit!"

Cops. Yeah, them. OK, the car you are driving is probably older than he or she is. Yeah, they seem to hassle us Old Farts less now than in our misspent youths. Still, this isn't a free ticket to speed. Use good judgement, especially in populated areas. Radar detectors actually work. Sometimes, what you may consider to be a perfectly acceptable rate of knots is somewhat faster than the Authorities believe is safe. A good radar detector can save you some financial grief.

If you are planning a group drive, the issue of safety and appropriate behavior needs to be addressed with everyone involved. These "Rules" obviously also apply if you are out on your own. Groups, however, magnify the problems. Most of us know the Rules without being told, but perhaps we need to think about them a little more seriously. So, what are the Rules for Engagement here? How do we balance our need for speed and enjoy a brisk drive, but not cross the line into surly arrogance? What does the Law say about it?

To this last end, in 2008, I had the opportunity to interview Officer Todd Workman of the California Highway Patrol's Altadena station. This is the station responsible for patrolling Angeles Crest so probably has the most experience in dealing with drivers (and motorcycle riders) who use roads as a playground. The drive/ride to Newcomb's Ranch for Sunday breakfast is a vastly enjoyable and easily accessible for most of us. He gave me some statistics. From 2003-2006, there were 419 collisions, 41 deaths, and 623 injuries. That's more than one death a month. On just one section alone, 116 collisions were reported for 2006. Prime causes were speed and crossing the double yellow line. OK class, can you guess what two things the CHP are going to focus on the most? They use radar up there, and from some turnouts, can tag you way down (or up) the hill, and wave you in when you arrive. If they see you *touch* the line, you're busted. There is one officer up there, who will write for everything and anything. *One* MPH over, busted. Full vehicle safety check while we are at it? Sure thing. He's got all day and a line up of cars and bikes to do. He doesn't really care how long it takes. Oh, and remember, Angeles Crest is a "Special Enforcement Zone," that means that traffic fines are *doubled.* I can't say that I blame the Chippies too much. Too many eedjits have gone "sailing on out there" in the past few years. A couple of years ago, not far from Newcomb's Ranch, I helped pull a guy's bike off the side of the mountain. He was lucky, just a bit shaken.

There are other issues as well. "Unsafe Speed." Even if you are below the speed limit it is the officer's call. Squealing tires, sideways drifting, hard braking, all these could apply. On top of that, and more germane to our concerns, is the issue of Street Racing. A group in a pack, exhibiting unsafe speed *could* be called a street race. *Minimum* $1000 fine, 30 day license suspension, and 30 day impound (in some yard where they have NO respect for your pride-and-joy) of your vehicle. To add insult to injury, this involves exorbitant towing and storage charges. Again, it's the officer's call. Some cities remember, will *seize and crush your car*!

So, what are the guidelines? Do we have to drive like white-knuckled little ol' ladies in tennis shoes? Can we push the limits a bit and still not act like jerks? Sure.

Road Trippin'

Rule #1: Use that most uncommon of all things, common sense. Duh! We are on open, public roads. To reiterate, there are no corner workers there to pull us out, or wave a yellow flag to warn us of what is around the next bend.

Rule #2: Stay well within your car's and your limits. Always keep something in reserve.

Rule #3: Stay on *your* friggin' side of the road! Granted, many of us fudge this at times. A long open stretch of esses, we want to take more of the racing line. Pick your spots *carefully* if you are so inclined, but know it *is* illegal and far less than safe.

Rule #4: Pass *only* using a passing lane. Yeah, its a pain to get stuck behind some cell phone yakking soccer mom who is afraid her SUV will roll over at anything over 15 mph and has *no* idea what a turnout is for. *Deal with it.* Hang back, and at some point, you'll get your chance.

Rule #5: Pull over for faster cars! Do unto others.

Rule #6: In Rural areas remember, if there are farm houses, there are people with phones. Blast by at 100+ in a pack and expect them to call the law (or worse, decide it's the day to take the tractor out and park it at the exit of a blind curve--that might *really* ruin your day). These folks *live* there. Their livestock is their income. Spook the cows or horses? They are gonna be righteously pissed. Maybe even 12 gauge pissed! Remember, they drive the roads *all the time*. That big ol' pick up of theirs can really fly. And by the way, if some cowboy on a horse is waving at you with his lasso, *stop!* He's not doing the Deliverance thing. He's telling you that up ahead, they are moving a whole freakin' herd of cattle up the road. "Boy, y'all hit one of them steers, it's gonna make a real mess o' yo' nice little car." We had this actually happen on our honeymoon on Foxen Canyon Road. We had ignored him, rounded the bend and there was a good 50 head coming our way. All I could say was "Yes, Sir, Sorry Sir."

Rule #7: If you over cook it, and take out some guys fence, man up. Find the owner or someone who lives near by. Tell 'em what stooopid thing you did, give them your insurance info and accept your fate. Remember, fences keep animals off the road. Exit a corner at speed and find 1000 pounds of potential pot roast in the way and things get ugly *real* fast. *By* the way, if a sign says "Free Range" or "Open Range" it doesn't mean that there is an oven waiting for pick up. It means there's *cattle out on the road--Be Careful.*

Rule #8: Don't ruin it for others. I first wrote up the "Rules" after the late, great, No Frills Iron Bottom Motoring Tour was disbanded a few years ago. There was a lot of anger and resentment over the demise of the Iron Bottom, caused in large part by a rogue squad of Road Nazis, blitzing in a wolf-pack at speeds in the mid triple digits. I remember talking later to one participant who sounded like he had lost a dear relation when he learned that future Iron Bottoms would be cancelled.

All in all, remember, organized drives are fun. They are a chance for us to escape and pretend that we are in the Miglia Mille. We get to see great scenery, get away from crowded freeways, enjoy good food and good company. We get to joke and BS each other. We don't want to get harassed or shepherded or out and out banned. Have Fun, Be Safe!

A Note About the Directions

Since we live in the San Gabriel Valley, northeast of LA, I've planned these trips to start from the Denny's Restaurant in Arcadia, just off the 210 Freeway, on the corner of Santa Anita Ave. and Huntington Drive. It's easy to find, there is a large parking lot if you're planning a group trip and although it violates my dictum on "No Corporate Food," Denny's does do a good cheap breakfast. There are also a couple of gas stations near by to top off the tank before you leave. You can obviously adjust your own directions accordingly.

I've tried to be consistent in presenting the directions. To me, the most sensible way is by listing the direction (left, right, etc or a compass direction if that is helpful) that you will be turning first, then the road, then the mileage until your next turning. All mileages are approximate, so stay alert. I tried to make sure everything makes sense, and apologize if you are led astray. I decided that including maps in this book wasn't worth the hassles, so bring a map and pay attention. If you get lost, remember, that's part of the adventure!

And by the way, in case you are wondering, Marianne and I are not arm chair Road Trippers. We have driven all of this. Not all in the TR3, to be sure (we did take the TR up to Washington one summer. Highway 101/1 all the way up!), so we don't just talk the talk, we drive the drive.

Long, Lonely, and straight, Route 66
photo by the author

California Coastal Trips

Some of the best roads in the western US involve the California Coast. The scenery is spectacular, the weather is pleasant (mostly), the food is good, and the roads are *great*. Spring is the best time of year, as the wildflowers are amazing, especially around the central coast. In summer, the traffic is heavier, and some of these areas can get extremely hot. Winter is when the rains come (maybe), but hey, its California, how bad can the weather get? What I've done in this chapter is to outline the first drive to Carpinteria, then do add ons and suggest alternates. These drives can be made into one day or multi-day trips, depending on your needs and the stamina of your backside. I also added a stand alone three day drive, based on the old Iron Bottom Tour. So get out there, and Go Coastal!

Spectacular California Coast, just south of Carpinteria
photo by the author

Carpinteria, the Back Way!

There are several neat towns to stop and check out along the way. Old Town Fillmore has some good eateries as does Santa Paula. Santa Paula also has a great little museum dedicated to the origins of the oil drilling industry. Ojai is a wonderful artsy community, but a bit yuppified for my taste. Still, you might want to check it out.

You can start anywhere you want, just adjust your mileages and your directions to the 118 Fwy. By the way: most drives require some freeways, especially to get out of town. It's unavoidable. This is one of our favorite drives. It's fairly easy (about 230 miles round trip) so have fun and stay safe!

Road Trippin'

Carpinteria-the Back Way-Directions

Now THAT's a Cruiser!
photo by Brianna McCarthy

NORTH on Santa Anita Ave	0.6 mi
RIGHT to merge onto I-210 W toward Pasadena	
Continue N/W on I-210 to La Canada	25.6 mi
WEST onto CA-118 W	27.5 mi
EXIT 19A-Princeton Ave	0.4 mi
LEFT on Princeton Ave	1.4 mi
CONTINUE on E. High St	0.4 mi
RIGHT on Moorpark Ave	500 ft
CONTINUE on CA-23 N	10.7 mi
LEFT on CA-126 W	
Continue to follow CA-126 W	8.8 mi
EXIT on CA-150/10th St	0.2 mi
RIGHT on S 10th St/CA-150 W	0.5 mi
Look for the Oil Museum on the right, it's in the old Union Oil company headquarters building.	
SLIGHT RIGHT on CA-150 W/N Ojai Rd	
Continue to follow CA-150 W	19.2 mi
RIGHT on Baldwin Rd/CA-150 W	
Continue to follow CA-150 W	15.1 mi
RIGHT on CA-192 W/Casitas Pass Rd	
Continue to follow CA-192 W	3.6 mi
LEFT on Linden Ave	

This is Downtown Carpinteria.

This is one of our favorite coastal towns. Parking in the summer may be an issue, so if you are planning to spend the day, the best be is to park at the state beach (one of the nicest beaches in California and a great place to camp, if you are so inclined) and walk back to town. There is public parking near the train station, but it's usually full, especially in the summer. either way, it's a short stroll. There are lots of antiques stores up and down Linden Ave., as well as on some of the side streets. The Worker Bee Cafe is a great place for breakfast and you can't beat The Spot for lunch. This is a classic burger stand that has been there *forever*. I ate there as a kid so it *must* be old! Tony's Pizza is another old favorite, and be sure and check out Robitaille's Candy Shop. If that name is familiar, the owner is the uncle of Luc Robitaille, hall of fame hockey player for the LA Kings. They are good enough to supply after dinner mints to the White House! The Palms is good for dinner and has rooms as well. There are several B&B's in town and even a decent Motel 6. In addition, there is a monthly flea market at the historical museum (check the museum's web site for details), and the city also puts on an annual car show.

To get home, the easy way is HWY 101 south through Ventura and back to LA. I recommend avoiding the San Fernando Valley and taking Hwy 126 back EAST from Ventura, then exit on 118 EAST in Saticoy, then follow it EAST to Moorpark where it joins the freeway (either 118 east or 23 south, depending where your actual starting point was). There are really good fruit and veggie stands on 118. Stop and pick up some for home. From there, take whatever variants you need to get you back.

Coastal Continuation--Pismo Beach

If you are up to a bit more adventure, this next bit is still within the realm of a one day drive. It's a bit longer, but easily doable without spending the night. More beach towns! More funky stuff, and good food to boot. Santa Barbara, Hope Ranch, Lompoc, Casmalia, Guadelupe, Oceano, and Pismo Beach. What's not to love? This adds about 125 miles from Carpinteria, so about 250 miles to a round trip. Obviously, you can head back at any point, just follow the 101 South. Santa Barbara has a wonderful art fair every Sunday. Obviously there is great food there as well. Further up the coast, in near Oceano are a couple of great places to eat. One is the Rusty Pig, a BBQ joint on the left at Halcyon Way. The other is a 50s style diner inside two railroad passenger cars called the Rock and Roll Diner. It will be on the left as you go, it's hard to miss! Guadelupe has some fine Mexican food, as well as the famous Far Western Tavern, This is a place you *have* to check out.

In and around Pismo, the traffic gets a bit thick, especially in the summer, so get into cruise mode for this part. Pismo also has regular arts and craft fairs in the summer so you might want to check these out.

Coastal Beauty!
photo by Marianne McCarthy

Coastal Continuation to Pismo Beach-Directions From Carpinteria:

NORTH on Linden Ave	0.7 mi
Continue straight onto CA-192 W/Foothill Rd	2.9 mi
RIGHT on Foothill Rd	1.5 mi
SLIGHT RIGHT on Toro Canyon Rd	0.6 mi
CONTINUE ON CA-192 W/E. Valley Rd	3.1 mi
LEFT on E Valley Rd	1.4 mi
RIGHT on CA-192 W/Sycamore Canyon Rd	1.7 mi
LEFT to stay on CA-192 W/Sycamore Canyon Rd	0.3 mi
LEFT on CA-144 S/Sycamore Canyon Rd	1.1 mi
At the traffic circle, take 3rd EXIT onto N Salinas St 0.4 mi	
RIGHT on Carpinteria St	0.5 mi
At the traffic circle, take 3rd EXIT onto S Milpas St	0.5 mi
RIGHT on E Cabrillo Blvd.	1.4 mi
CONTINUE on Shoreline Dr.	1.9 mi
CONTINUE on Meigs Rd	0.4 mi
LEFT on Cliff Dr.	2.1 mi
LEFT on Marina Dr.	0.9 mi
CONTINUE on Roble Dr.	0.4 mi
CONTINUE on Las Palmas Dr.	0.5 mi
RIGHT to stay on Las Palmas Dr.	1.9 mi
RIGHT on Calle Real	0.3 mi
RIGHT to merge onto CA-1 N/US-101 N	30.8 mi
EXIT CA-1 to Lompoc/Vandenberg AFB	0.3 mi
LEFT on CA-1 N	17.9 mi
LEFT on E. Ocean Ave	1.3 mi
RIGHT on N. H St	2.7 mi
LEFT on CA-1 N/Cabrillo Hwy	6.6 mi
RIGHT on Co Rd 20	2.6 mi
SHARP LEFT on San Antonio Rd W	2.8 mi
CONTINUE on W. Lompoc Casmalia Rd	4.4 mi
CONTINUE on Black Rd	3.7 mi
LEFT on CA-1 N/Cabrillo Hwy	
Continue to follow CA-1 N	24.1 mi
RIGHT on Pismo Ave	

This is Pismo Beach.

Pismo has a lot to offer. Good food abounds as well as a wide range of places to stay. Everything from Motel 6 to luxury spas. Triple A has some good recommendations. Overall, not a bad place to stop for the night after a long day in the saddle. On top of that, the beaches are generally cleaner and less crowded than the usual spots in LA or OC. If you are heading back, take Hwy 101 south. That will get you to the major freeways in LA.

California Coast-Alternate Routes

Now, in no way are the above routes the only way to go and have fun along the coast. Back more years than either of us would admit, my buddy Bill Morgan and I, avid *Road & Track* readers and wanna be racers, read an article in *R&T* about the best drives in southern California. Naturally, we had to try them. Needless to say, these roads were a revelation. We were both about 22, mere callow youths, and set out in either the TR3 (yes, I've had the Blue Meanie *that* long), or in his Spitfire (which ever car was running) and went in search of those sacred trails. WOW. All I can say, is WOW! The mists of memory and that ever present rosy glow of nostalgia give a mythical quality to these, our first Road Loves, but even today, they rank as some of the best drives around. In the intervening years, more people have learned about this back country, mostly north of Santa Barbara, so traffic is a bit heavier. In addition, wineries have also spouted like weeds in the area which is a two edged sword. Always great to stop and get some good wine, not so good to do much tasting and then flog the back roads. Doubly not so good sharing the road with those who have tasted too much! These are roads to stay away from on a weekend or the summer. In the off season, they are still great. They are *the* Classic SoCal Back Roads!

We'll again pick up from Carpinteria (actually, Hwys 126, 150, and 192 were part of these classic roads) and head to Los Olivos, Los Alamos, and Solvang.

View from the navigator's seat--
Bitterwater Road near Paso Robles
photo by Marianne McCarthy

Coastal Alternates-Directions From Carpinteria:

NORTH on Linden Ave toward Carpinteria Ave	0.7 mi
CONTINUE STRAIGHT on CA-192 W/Foothill Rd	2.9 mi
RIGHT on Foothill Rd	1.5 mi
SLIGHT RIGHT on Toro Canyon Rd	0.6 mi
CONTINUE on CA-192 W/E Valley Rd	3.1 mi
LEFT on E Valley Rd	1.4 mi
RIGHT on CA-192 W/Sycamore Canyon Rd	1.7 mi
LEFT to stay on CA-192 W/Sycamore Canyon Rd	0.3 mi
RIGHT on Foothill Rd/Stanwood Dr	
Continue to follow Stanwood Dr	0.7 mi
TAKE 2nd LEFT to stay on Stanwood Dr	0.8 mi
RIGHT on Mission Ridge Rd	0.3 mi
SLIGHT LEFT on Mountain Dr	0.4 mi
SECOND RIGHT on CA-192 W/Foothill Rd	3.8 mi
RIGHT to merge onto CA-154 W/San Marcos Pass Rd	4.8 mi
RIGHT on Painted Cave Rd.	3.1 mi

VERY TIGHT AND TWISTY AND NARROW!
      Look for the Chumash cave paintings!

CONTINUE on E Camino Cielo/Forest Route 5N12	2.1 mi
RIGHT on Stagecoach Rd	213 ft
RIGHT to stay on Stagecoach Rd	5.2 mi

      Look for Cold Spring Tavern. Once a stage stop on the way to
      Santa Barbara before the railroad connected at Goleta.

RIGHT on CA-154 W/San Marcos Pass Rd	17.6 mi

      This is Los Olivos. Look for Mattie's Tavern, another stage stop
      to connect the railroad to Santa Barbara and the Southern Pacific RR.

WEST on CA-154 W/Calkins Rd/San Marcos Pass Rd toward Grand Ave	3.2 mi
RIGHT on Zaca Canyon Rd/Zaca Station Rd	3.1 mi
CONTINUE STRAIGHT on Foxen Canyon Rd	15.8 mi
RIGHT to stay on Foxen Canyon Rd	1.1 mi
CONTINUE on Foxen Cny Rd	0.2 mi
LEFT on Palmer Rd	6.6 mi
LEFT on US-101 S	2.9 mi
SLIGHT RIGHT toward Bell St	0.2 mi
CONTINUE STRAIGHT on Bell St	1.5 mi

This is Los Alamos.
Look for the Depot Antiques Mall.
This was part of one of California's few narrow gauge railroads.
Directions continued next page

Road Trippin'

From the Depot:

HEAD BACK WEST Toward Centennial St.

LEFT on Centennial St	0.4 mi
CONTINUE on Drum Canyon Rd	9.0 mi
TIGHT AND TWISTY!	
LEFT on CA-246 E	6.0 mi
RIGHT to merge onto El Camino Real/US-101 S	4.8 mi
LEFT on La Lata Pl (Look for signs for Nojoqui Park)	1.0 mi
FIRST LEFT on Alisal Rd	7.3 mi
RIGHT on Mission Dr	

This is Solvang.

It's a touristy, but charming Danish-American community. Get abelskiver! Get REAL Danish! Check out Mission Santa Ynez. From Solvang, it's easy to either get back to Santa Barbara via 101 or 154, or head further north. The hotels in Solvang are pretty good and so's the food. Summer is *crowded* though. Also, check the calendar and phone ahead. You *do not* want to be there during their two big bicycle rides!

The Blue Meanie powering out
of a sweeper
photo by Mike Andrews

Route of the Late, Lamented, No-Frills-Iron-Bottom-Motoring-Tour

Now if you already know about the Iron Bottom, you know that this was the most fun a body could ever have (with one's clothes on, at least). Three days of blasting around some of the finest back roads on the planet! One Thousand Miles of gut wrenching, butt pounding, unadulterated *fun*! I thought it would be a good idea to let readers who never took part in the Iron Bottom to get an idea of the roads the Immortal Disorganizers planned out. The day one route is just under 300 miles of really fine roads and scenery that highlight California as one of the premier places to drive on the planet. Anybody know how to induce, kidnap, or otherwise force Wanker, Pillock, and Pratt, those anti-American hosts of *Top Gear* to get their butts behind the wheel over here? It would put to rest the notion that the US (and California in particular) is nothing but freeways, hoards of people, and Mickey D's.

The Iron Bottom (as most folks called it) was the brain child (well maybe sick and twisted stepchild) of Ed Pasini and Jack Brown. Ed and Jack and a few others thought the high-falutin'-multi-thousand-dollar-luxury-tours-for-high-rollers-and-their-mega-buck-ego-rides was not what back road motoring should be about. Some of those tours have highway patrol escorts. Sheesh, where's the fun in *that*? Ed figured that the ultimate anti-big buck tour was needed, so he put together a tour with the simple motto: "No Frills!" and that's just what it was. You showed up at the Rose Bowl before 7 am, got a route book and you were on your own. The one major rule was that there *were* no rules, other than use a bit of common sense. Make your own reservations in Paso Robles for two nights, stop when you needed gas, food or a pee, drive at whatever pace tickled your Elmo, pay your own tickets, and have fun. The route was really a suggestion. Ed figured we were all big girls and boys and didn't need a den mother.

For the last one (2008) over 100 cars (almost all pre-1976) started. Everything from a 1930 Lagonda, previously owned by Gary Cooper, to a 914 Porsche with a 935 engine in it. There are usually a few TRs, Alfas, and MGs, all in various states of appearance, Ed's old 356 Porsche, DS21 Citroens, a Packard 120, a Lambo Miura, took part. There was even an Olds Vista Cruiser that set up each night in the parking lot at the motel as a bar car. One year, a *real* masochist ran a Citroen Mihari. We've been sun burned, snowed on and rained on, all in one tour. We've limped the Blue Meanie home from Hollister with a completely broken rear leaf spring. We've suffered the Bar Car's Everclear Margueritas, and paused a moment at the James Dean Memorial. We've had nothing but fun the whole time.

The route was never exactly the same, but there were some expected roads people really enjoyed. Usually, we led off with Angeles Crest/Angeles Forest Hwy, then up Lake Elizabeth Road. Some years we headed through Frazier Park, others, across 126 to Santa Paula, then 33 over Wheeler Ridge from Ojai. Highway 58 over to the coast was another road we often took, then a few oddities before getting to Paso Robles. Day Two took us up to Monterey and Hollister, along the absolutely gorgeous Carmel Valley Road, and Highway 25. We wound up back in Paso for the night. Next morning it was off for home, suffering the roads of the coastal range. You haven't lived until you've descended Naciemento-Ferguson Road. There was usually a stretch of the Legendary Highway 1 and believe me there is nothing like slipstreaming an Aston-Martin DB4 at 5500 rpm in 4th overdrive down Highway 1. I'll let you do the math on that one.

Like all car-oriented escapades, it was the people who really made the Iron Bottom worth the pain and suffering. Snobs didn't do the Iron Bottom. Everyone was a genuine Car Guy/Gal. Everybody changed their own oil and got their hands dirty. Everyone had more than a few good tales to tell, and naturally wasn't shy about telling them. This was a crowd from the Good Old Days when cars were Fun and not an Investment. These were people who believed that cars are meant to be driven, not stared at in a museum. There were no Trailer Queens, no pretensions, and no worries. There were also no special t-shirts, no dash plaques, and best of all, no rules. The route was a suggestion. Plenty of people found side roads (some dirt, look for Old Hernandez Rd), everyone went their own pace. This drive lasted ten years and then it suffered from its own popularity. Sadly, some jerks thought it was a race. Mid-Triple Digits on the speedo were posted on the internet. The reality of liability began to rear its ugly head and Ed and Jack pulled the plug.

**Chasing Chuck and Tina of Autobooks in their Cute little Alfa
photo by Marianne McCarthy**

Time of year plays a role in this drive. Spring is best as the hills are covered with a velvety green, and quilted with orange, yellow, and purple wildflowers. It can also be wet. Very Wet. One year it poured all three days. One year, it wasn't even foggy in Monterey! Summer is Hot. Really Hot! In the 100s except right along the coast. Plan accordingly, and bring water for the car and yourselves. There is a bunch of hill climbing, so your Auld Crate may not be too happy at times. Bring a blanket and some shade and some food for an impromptu picnic if you need to cool things down. In Fall, there is a nice crispness to the air, but some days can still be pretty warm. Winter is a real throw of the dice. Snow on Angeles Crest and Frazier Park, rain around Paso Robles. Check the weather reports before you go, and it would be a good idea to take (gulp) chains.

There are some cool sights to see as well. Jack Ranch is a pretty good place to eat and is the site of the James Dean Memorial, and when you see the signs for Parkfield, turn right to get to the town. Its also got good food and some odd fountains. It's also the Earthquake Capital of California. Those huge chasms you've crossed, yeah, that's *the* San Andreas Fault. Pretty spectacular picture spots. By The Way, unless you like dirt roads, don't continue north out of Parkfield. Turn around and go back to pick up the route.

In Paso Robles, we usually stayed at the Motel 6. It's cheap and decent and leaves the wallet with more dough for gas (uggh, Don't let's get started on *that* topic) and food. The Iron Bottom was usually headquartered at the Black Oak which is very nice. If you turn right out of the parking lot of the Black Oak, then left on Spring St., you will get to Downtown Paso Robles. Turn left on 12th St. and you will find a pleasant little park. There are a number of very good places to eat in this area. We always get a scoop (pint of Guinness) or two at the Crooked Kilt. Their Shepard's pie and fish and chips (get the *garlic* fries with that---oooooooooBABY) are fantastic, the service is great and they sometimes have a traditional Irish music group playing. Its like the den we all wish we had! The waitresses are also easy on the eyes.

This drive lasted ten years and then it suffered from its own popularity. The reality of liability began to rear its ugly head and Ed and Jack pulled the plug.

The Iron Bottom traditionally started at the Rose Bowl in Pasadena, so, for sentiment's sake, I'll start you off from there as well.

The Last Iron Bottom Logo
Art Work by Mike Andrews

Road Trippin'

Iron Bottom-Day One

HEAD NORTHEAST on Seco St toward Lincoln Ave	0.4 mi
CONTINUE on W Mountain St	0.1 mi
LEFT to merge onto I-210 W toward San Fernando	3.9 mi
TAKE the CA-2/Angeles Crest Hwy exit toward La Cañada Flintridge	0.4 mi
RIGHT on Angeles Crest Hwy/CA-2 N	9.2 mi
LEFT on Angeles Forest Hwy	24.6 mi
RIGHT on Sierra Hwy	0.3 mi
LEFT to merge onto CA-14 N toward Palmdale	4.9 mi
TAKE EXIT 35 for CA-138 E/Palmdale Blvd. toward Palmdale	0.3 mi
LEFT on E Palmdale Blvd.	1.0 mi
CONTINUE on Elizabeth Lake Rd	15.0 mi
LEFT to stay on Elizabeth Lake Rd	4.6 mi
CONTINUE on Pine Canyon Rd	9.6 mi
LEFT to stay on Pine Canyon Rd	7.4 mi
RIGHT to stay on Pine Canyon Rd	0.6 mi
FIRST RIGHT on Co Route N2/Old Ridge Route/Ridge Route Rd	2.2 mi
LEFT on CA-138 W/Lancaster Rd	2.5 mi
RIGHT on Gorman Post Rd	259 ft
LEFT to stay on Gorman Post Rd	4.8 mi
LEFT on Gorman School Rd	325 ft
RIGHT to merge onto I-5 N	2.5 mi
TAKE EXIT 205 for Frazier Mountain Park Rd	0.3 mi
LEFT on Frazier Mountain Park Rd	7.2 mi
CONTINUE on Cuddy Valley Rd	5.0 mi
SLIGHT RIGHT on Forest Route 9N05/Mil Potrero Hwy	
Continue to follow Mil Potrero Hwy	8.2 mi
CONTINUE on Cerro Noroeste Rd	21.3 mi
RIGHT on CA-166 E/CA-33 N Continue to follow CA-166 E/CA-33 N	9.2 mi
LEFT on CA-33 N/California St/West Side Hwy Continue to follow CA-33 N	6.3 mi
LEFT to stay on CA-33 N/West Side Hwy	15.6 mi
SHARP LEFT on CA-58 W	10.5 mi
RIGHT on CA-58 W/Santa Maria Valley Hwy	2.6 mi
RIGHT on CA-58 W Continue to follow CA-58 W/Carrisa Hwy	16.9 mi
LEFT to stay on Hwy/CA-58 W/Carrisa Hwy	3.1 mi
RIGHT on Bitterwater Rd	20.8 mi
CONTINUE on Annette Rd/Palo Prieto Rd Continue to follow Annette Rd.	1.6 mi
LEFT on Bitterwater Rd	9.1 mi
LEFT on CA-41 S/CA-46 W	
Continue to follow CA-46 W. Hotels are just west of Hwy 101	23.0 mi

This is Paso Robles

Iron Bottom, Day Two

The day two route is a "simple" up and back, so at least you can leave most of your stuff in the motel. It covers over 350 miles, so its a long day. This is also my favorite part of the drive. All of the roads are wonderful. The scenery is terrific and runs the full gamut from coastal grassy fields with oak trees, to pine forests, to the almost desert-like, to the cool and usually foggy coast. Its a real microcosm of California. A number of these roads have also been included on several magazine top-ten lists.

Food is another area of interest on Day Two. There are several ways to handle this. Personally, my wife and I enjoy the liberty of a simple picnic lunch. A baguette, a chub of Gallo dry Italian salami, some Swiss cheese and we are set. On road trips, we keep to Cokes or water and hold the beer/wine for the end of the day. These roads are a challenge and you need to be on top of things. Even one beer can put you off your game at just the wrong time. There are plenty of places to stop and enjoy along the way. Pick a shady turnout and relax. Just be sure to clean up after yourself. In years past, the Iron Bottom stopped for picnic lunch at the Hollister Off Road Park, but it costs money. That and the bad memory of breaking a rear leaf spring there one year (and yes, we limped home after some repairs that involved tying the axle to the frame) so we stay away. Another option is a Subway Sandwich Shop in Coalinga (you *really* want to gas up here). I'll include it in the directions. By the way, ever wonder how Coalinga got its name? No, its *not* Spanish for anything. It was originally a refueling stop on the Southern Pacific. "Coaling A" was the only identifying name it got. Run it together--Coalinga. A third option is San Juan Bautista. Its a neat little town with some good restaurants. Chuck and Tina recommend Joan & Peter's German Restaurant. There is also a Basque eatery in town called Matxain Etxea that looks promising. Add to that some good shopping for antiques and a couple of great jewelry places. Marianne and Tina both scored big on turquoise one year. And just to make it a perfect rest stop, add an ice cream parlor and the mission. Be careful, during the school year, the place is over run with 4th graders doing the California Mission thing--Tina got the heebie-jeebies at the mere *thought* of bus loads of 9 year olds in such close proximity. The square in front of the mission is also a good place to picnic. The kids are usually gone by noon or so. Check out the view of the San Andreas Fault. Its also the locale of the final scene of "Vertigo," but there is no bell tower on the real mission.

Back on the road and on to Monterey. Its a bit of stop and go, and there is a bit of freeway involved, but Carmel Valley Road is worth it. This road is drop dead gorgeous! Oak forests and Spanish moss, dark shadows and bright sun. This road gets seriously twisty and narrow, but man is it worth it. From there, its back to 101 and a relaxing cruise back to Paso Robles.

Road Trippin'

Iron Bottom, Day Two

HEAD NORTH on US-101 N	6.9 mi
TAKE EXIT 239A for Mission St	0.2 mi
RIGHT on Mission St	0.8 mi
TAKE 3rd RIGHT on 14th St	361 ft
CONTINUE on N River Rd	0.5 mi
LEFT on Cross Canyon Rd/Cross Canyons Rd	0.1 mi
FIRST LEFT on Indian Valley Rd	1.4 mi
RIGHT on Vineyard Canyon Rd	16.7 mi
RIGHT to stay on Vineyard Canyon Rd	4.4 mi
LEFT on 1st St/Parkfield-Coalinga Rd	1.7 mi
LEFT to stay on Parkfield-Coalinga Rd	6.1 mi
LEFT to stay on Parkfield-Coalinga R	3.2 mi
CONTINUE on Parkfield Grade	1.3 mi
RIGHT to stay on Parkfield Grade	
SHARP RIGHT on CA-198 E	9.8 mi
LEFT on W Polk St	

This is Coalinga   0.9 mi

    The Subway Sandwich place is on the left in the shopping center.
    There is also a market there. Gas up in Coalinga!!

CONTINUE on Jayne Ave	0.5 mi
CONTINUE on S Derrick Ave	4.0 mi
LEFT on Los Gatos Rd/Coalinga Rd	6.8 mi
FIRST LEFT on Los Gatos Rd/Coalinga Rd	21.6 mi
CONTINUE on Coalinga Rd	24.1 mi
SLIGHT RIGHT on Airline Hwy	249 ft
CONTINUE on Coalinga Rd	0.9 mi
RIGHT on Airline Hwy/CA-25 N	24.8 mi
LEFT on Old Airport Rd	0.3 mi
FIRST RIGHT to stay on Old Airport Rd	2.0 mi
LEFT on Cienega Rd	1.0 mi
RIGHT to stay on Cienega Rd	14.0 mi
LEFT to stay on Cienega Rd	1.4 mi
LEFT on Union Rd	3.6 mi
LEFT on CA-156 W/San Juan Rd	4.2 mi
RIGHT on The Alameda	0.2 mi
CONTINUE on 3rd St	0.2 mi
RIGHT on Polk St	259 ft
FIRST LEFT on 2nd St	

This is San Juan Bautista Directions for after lunch in San Juan Bautista on next page

Iron Bottom, Day Two, Continued
After Lunch-

HEAD NORTHWEST on 2nd St toward Muckelemi St	230 ft
FIRST LEFT on Muckelemi St	0.4 mi
LEFT on Monterey St	276 ft
FIRST RIGHT on CA-156 W	2.5 mi
TAKE RAMP FOR CA-156 W/El Camino Real/US-101 S	8.5 mi
TAKE EXIT toward Monterey/Peninsula	0.4 mi
MERGE onto CA-156 W	6.1 mi
CONTINUE on CA-1 S	12.6 mi
EXIT onto CA-68 E/Monterey Salinas Hwy/Salinas Hwy toward Salinas	
Continue to follow CA-68 E/Monterey Salinas Hwy	7.5 mi
RIGHT on Laureles Grade	5.9 mi
LEFT on W Carmel Valley Rd/Co Rd G16	22.3 mi
RIGHT on E Carmel Valley Rd/Co Rd G16/Jamesburg-Arroyo Seco Rd	
Continue to follow E Carmel Valley Rd/Co Rd G16	8.4 mi
CONTINUE on Arroyo Seco Rd	6.5 mi
SLIGHT RIGHT on Co Rd G16/Elm Ave	0.2 mi
RIGHT to stay on Co Rd G16/Elm Ave	3.7 mi
RIGHT on Central Ave	7.1 mi
LEFT to stay on Central Ave	0.1 mi
FIRST RIGHT onto US-101 S	54.4 mi
TAKE EXIT 231B for CA-46 E toward Fresno/Bakersfield	

This is Paso Robles. Again.

There are other roads to explore along 101. Check a good map and have fun.

Yeah, that's SNOW!
Gets cold in the TR
sometimes!
Above Fraizier Park on
the Iron Bottom
photo by Marianne
McCarthy

Iron Bottom--Day Three

There are a number of options here, depending on just how iron your bottom is. You may want to cut some of this short, I've added a few incredible roads, some pretty famous around here, some not, and some already mentioned in conjunction with other routes. As always, here are some notes and warnings and suggestions.

Number One: The first part of this route takes you through Hunter-Liggett Army Base. Now, I hope that the mere thought of uniforms and guns doesn't make you break out in a rash, but relax. Unlike my first trips up to Laguna Seca Raceway for the CanAm races in the 60s and 70s, when the track was in the middle of Fort Ord, there is no draft, so the Army isn't going to grab you and pressgang you into service. Not that they'd want most of us today. Anyway, access to the base *requires* that you have a driver's license (for everybody in the car-or at least a picture ID), registration, and proof of insurance ready at the gate. You're going in one side and out the other. You may want to stop and see Mission San Antonio while you're there. It's also where William Randolph Hearst maintained a hunting lodge. It's the Spanish styled building to the right before you get to the mission. He owned everything up there as his ranch. All the way down to San Simeon. Ya gotta wonder what the poor people are doing! By the way, this *is* an active training base. Keep the speed down, there are troops out on training maneuvers all over the place. It's pretty interesting. Give them a wave, they deserve it.

Number Two: Naciemento-Fergueson Road is a gold plated horror story of a road. Its fun, but a workout and a half. Take it easy, save your brakes, and enjoy the view. It is spectacular and worth every twist and turn.

Number Three: Gas in Cambria is expensive! The bright side is that there are plenty of good places to eat there and along the way. Be careful of the antiques stores. Your significant other/passenger for life may want to stop. Never a problem in the TR3, there's not enough room for anything really expensive.

Number Four: There are also good places to eat up (down?) the road in both Cayucos and Morro Bay. Excellent fish is to be had if you go waaay down the wharf area in Morro Bay to the north. Its a bit more off the tourist path.

Number Five: Solvang gets crowded, but its fun. Stop at the Solvang Bakery or get some of Arnies Abelskeber. AAAAHHHH GOOD.

Number Six: At several points long the way, the route crisscrosses Hwy 101. Obviously, use it to head home at whatever point you get tired. You will probably note a few roads we've used before, so some of this should be familiar territory.

Enjoy the drive, and safe home to you.

Iron Bottom-Day Three

RIGHT on 24th St	0.8 mi
CROSS Spring St.	
SLIGHT RIGHT on Nacimiento Lake Dr/Paso Robles Rd	7.5 mi
RIGHT on Godfrey Rd/Nacimiento Lake Dr	7.6 mi
RIGHT to stay on Nacimiento Lake Dr	1.7 mi
LEFT on Interlake Rd	20.4 mi
LEFT on Co Rd G14/Jolon Rd	5.9 mi
LEFT on Mission Rd	3.1 mi
LEFT on Nacimiento-Fergusson Rd	0.8 mi
LEFT to stay on Nacimiento-Fergusson Rd	24.2 mi
RIGHT on CA-1 S/Cabrillo Hwy	41.9 mi
LEFT on Weymouth St	0.2 mi
RIGHT on Charing Ln	0.3 mi
CONTINUE on Main St	1.8 mi
LEFT on Santa Rosa Creek Rd	6.9 mi
RIGHT on Santa Rosa Creek Rd	9.4 mi
CONTINUE on Old Creek Rd	9.1 mi
LEFT on CA-1 S/Cabrillo Hwy	4.0 mi
TAKE EXIT 279A for Main St	0.2 mi
RIGHT on Main St	3.2 mi
RIGHT on S Bay Blvd.	1.4 mi
LEFT on Turri Rd	2.5 mi
RIGHT to stay on Turri Rd	2.1 mi
LEFT on Los Osos Valley Rd	7.2 mi
LEFT on S Higuera St	0.4 mi
RIGHT on Tank Farm Rd	1.7 mi
RIGHT on Broad St/CA-227 S	9.5 mi
LEFT on Corbett Canyon Rd	0.6 mi
RIGHT on E Branch St	0.8 mi
LEFT on Traffic Way	0.5 mi
TAKE RAMP onto US-101 S	40.1 mi
TAKE CA-154 ramp to Los Olivos/Lake Cachuma	0.3 mi
LEFT on CA-154/San Marcos Pass Rd	32.6 mi
LEFT to merge onto US-101 S	34.8 mi
SLIGHT RIGHT at CA-126 E (signs for CA HWY126 E)	5.3 mi
TAKE EXIT 5 for Wells Rd/CA-118 toward Saticoy	0.3 mi
RIGHT on CA-118 E/S Continue to follow CA-118 E	3.5 mi
LEFT on CA-118 E/W Los Angeles Ave	14.5 mi
RIGHT to merge onto CA-118 E	28.0 mi
EAST on I-210 E toward Pasadena	18.3 mi

NoCal Coastal Drives

"Go north, young man, go north." Well, not exactly Horace Greeley's famous words, but they fit this road trip. We SoCal folk rarely take the time and trouble to head towards the neat roads of our NoCal brethren. So, put on your Dodger's gear (they *really* hate that--if they get snippy, just ask how many World Series the Giants have won since moving west) and head for the Bay Area however you want to. I'll be giving directions from Frisco (they also *love* it when we call "The City" that, heeheehee) but you can stay any place easy up there. We stayed with daughter #2 in Pleasant Hill, one of those east bay communities, but you actually might want to check out Martinez. Its a gem of a town with some decent eateries. Try the Bulldog BBQ in the old town section. Very Good. In fact, they have a cute old town that is worth checking out. I'm giving the directions from the Super 8 in Martinez, you can figure your own way from other towns.

No matter which way you go, north from Frisco across the Golden Gate Bridge or South from San Rafael, exit 101 toward Stinson Beach, CA-1. Yep, THAT CA-1. It really does go further north than Monterey. From Hwy 1, you will be looking for signs for Pt. Reyes National Seashore, Inverness, and Tomales State Park. Google won't tell you how to get out to the lighthouse so I inserted the directions at the appropriate place. By the way, on a weekend in particular, bicyclists are fairly thick so watch out for them and Share The Road! Inverness has some neat looking places to eat, and oysters are the thing to get. Slurp down a few for brunch. Pt. Reyes is neat, but probably foggy. The road out and back is a lot of fun, but remember, you are dealing with U.S. Park Rangers. There are also active ranches (dating from the 1850s no less) and free range cattle so watch it. Once you get to the parking for the lighthouse, there is a short walk to the visitor's center. The walk down to the lighthouse itself is a challenge. Note the sign that advises that the stairs are the equivalent of a 30 story building. Don't say I didn't warn you. This side trip is worth it, especially if the day is clear. Lots of cool Nature Stuff. When you've had enough, head back the same road back to Hwy One and turn left.

The town of Pt. Reyes Station looks worth exploring but you may want to make some time. Bodega Bay is the next town of any size and there are more places to eat there as well. From there, the next stop is Guerneville (my mom always pronounced the second "e," as in Gurney-ville, but a lot of people will say it without that "e"--Guern-ville. Take your pick, you're sure to irritate *someone* no matter what) and we had great luck there. On Saturdays there is a swap meet in the Safeway Market parking lot. Mostly junk, but we found a guy who is there every week selling very good turquoise. You probably remember Marianne's obsession, right? Since it was our anniversary (#29, thank you very much), I got her a gorgeous bracelet. All together now, *ahh, how sweet.* Before you turn off for Guerneville, you might want to take the time to keep going north to Ft. Ross. This was a Russian outpost back in the early 1800s. Its a great little park and a fascinating place to visit.

Once out of G-Ville, you are headed towards 101, and will cross it to head over the hill to Calistoga. Another neat road and there are plenty of options if you are interested. There are also lots of wineries. Stop and taste, but *be careful*. Even a few sips can add up. There is also a for real Petrified Forest (which is why, I guess, they named the road Petrified Forest Road. Just a guess mind you), it's interesting in a funky way. Check it out. Calistoga is chock-a-block full of great places to stay. The Hydro Bar in Calistoga has good eats and drinks. In fact, the bar not only has a fine selection of malt whiskies, it carries McCarthy's! You know that has to be good stuff! My buddy Bill calls the place his office.

Ask for him and he'll make you buy him a 7&7. We used to love Nances Hot Springs, but its been "renovated," so I'm not sure how good it is. Give it a try anyway. The Calistoga Inn is a great place to eat or really treat yourself and head down the valley to Younteville and the French Laundry. It "only" has one Michelin Star, so it can't cost *that* much, can it? The El Bonita Motel in St. Helena is a nicely refurbished old style motel. In the summer, make sure you have reservations for rooms, Napa Valley is *crammed*. Better to hit it in the spring of fall. Also, make sure you have room for wine in the trunk.

I've added a Day Two to the original drive. It will take you from Calistoga up to Mendocino, by way of Booneville (don't let 'em know that you're a brightlighter pikin' down the mason-dixon--there is an actual language called Boontling that the locals made up about 100 years ago), then over to Clear Lake and back to Calistoga. This is a truly great drive in and of itself. About 280 miles of pretty twisty stuff. You could stay the night in Mendocino if you want to do more wineries and such. A word of advice, DO NOT GET GAS IN MENDOCINO! Its insanely expensive. If you can plan it to get to Ft. Bragg, do it there. Speaking of Ft. Bragg, You could add more to the trip and keep heading north on Hwy 1 to where it joins 101 and head back 101. This is also spectacular, but be warned, the top part of Hwy 1 is *real* twisty.

Normally fog shrouded Golden Gate Bridge
photo by Marianne McCarthy

27

Road Trippin'

NoCal Coastal Trip-Directions From Martinez, CA:

SOUTH on Alhambra Ave	0.2 mi
Merge WEST on CA-4 W via the ramp to Richmond	8.1 mi
EXIT on I-80 W toward San Francisco	9.4 mi
EXIT Carlson Blvd	0.2 mi
RIGHT on Carlson Blvd	0.4 mi
LEFT on Bayview Ave	0.1 mi
RIGHT to merge onto I-580 W toward San Rafael	
Partial toll road	9.4 mi
EXIT on Sir Francis Drake Blvd	1.9 mi
MERGE South onUS-101 S	
via the ramp on the left to San Francisco	4.5 mi
Take the CA-1 exit toward Stinson Beach	0.3 mi
Turn left at CA-1/Shoreline Hwy	0.5 mi
Turn left to stay on CA-1/Shoreline Hwy	1.2 mi
Turn left to stay on CA-1/Shoreline Hwy	26.0 mi
Turn left at Sir Francis Drake Blvd.	5.2 mi
Turn right at Camino del Mar	

Follow the signs for the Lighthouse. The drive is about 19 miles out to the point.

Head southwest on Camino del Mar toward Sir Francis Drake Blvd.

Turn left at Sir Francis Drake Blvd.	5.2 mi
Turn left at CA-1/Shoreline Hwy	0.2 mi
Turn left at A St/CA-1	
Continue to follow CA-1	22.0 mi
Turn left at CA-1/Valley Ford Rd	
Continue to follow CA-1	19.7 mi
Slight right at CA-116	27.8 mi
Continue on Mark W Springs Rd	5.3 mi
Continue on Porter Creek Rd	4.7 mi
Turn left at Petrified Forest Rd	4.4 mi
Turn right at CA-128/Foothill Blvd.	1.0 mi
Turn left at CA-29/Lincoln Ave.	0.3 mi

This is Calistoga, CA

HEAD NORTH on CA-128 W/Foothill Blvd.	17.4 mi
TURN RIGHT to stay on CA-128 W	1.8 mi
TURN RIGHT to stay on CA-128 W	0.3 mi
TAKE 1st LEFT to stay on CA-128 W	3.7 mi
TURN LEFT to stay on CA-128 W	0.9 mi
RIGHT on CA-128 W/Geyserville Ave	0.9 mi
LEFT on CA-128 W/Canyon Rd (signs for State Hwy 128/US-101)	344 ft
RIGHT to merge onto US-101 N toward Eureka	10.0 mi
EXIT on CA-128 W toward Ft Bragg/Mendocino	0.2 mi
LEFT on CA-128 W/N Redwood Hwy	0.8 mi

TAKE 2nd RIGHT onto CA-128 W/(signs for Ft Bragg/Mendocino)

Continue to follow CA-128   55.4 mi

CONTINUE STRAIGHT onto CA-1 N/Shoreline Hwy   10.4 mi

LEFT on Little Lake Rd   0.2 mi

RIGHT on Lansing St   0.1 mi

This is Mendocino. Great places to eat and shops to visit.

To leave town:

Head North on Lansing St.   0.7 mi

LEFT on CA-1 N/Shoreline Hwy   7.2 mi

RIGHT on CA-20 E/Fort Bragg-Willits Rd (signs for State Route 20)

Continue to follow CA-20 E   33.1 mi

RIGHT on US-101 S   15.6 mi

TAKE EXIT 555B to merge onto CA-20 E toward Upper Lake/Williams 19.5 mi

RIGHT on CA-29 S   11.0 mi

This is Clear Lake

CONTINUE to follow CA-29 S   14.2 mi

CONTINUE onto Co Rd 140/Main St   14.2 mi

CONTINUE on Berryessa Knoxville Rd/Knoxville Rd   23.1 mi

RIGHT on Pope Canyon Rd   8.4 mi

RIGHT on Pope Valley Cross Rd   1.0 mi

RIGHT on Chiles Pope Valley Rd/Pope Valley Rd   0.8 mi

SLIGHT LEFT on Howell Mountain Rd   5.9 mi

CONTINUE on Deer Park Rd   4.7 mi

RIGHT on CA-128 W/CA-29 N/St Helena Hwy

     Continue to follow CA-128 W/CA-29 N   6.8 mi

RIGHT on Lincoln Ave   0.2 mi

TAKE 3rd LEFT onto Washington St   210 ft

You are back in Calistoga. To get home, follow 29 south and the signs for the various Bay Area interstates.

The Faithful Blue Meanie,
photo by Marianne McCarthy

Miscellaneous California Trips

Not all the great roads in California are on the coast. There are several inland routes that offer great drives and wonderful stuff to see, do, and eat. Here's a few of our favorites. The initial drive is a bit of a hodgepodge and can be taken in small chunks or put together. The first part is a nice drive for just a couple of hours. The second part would make a decent day trip on its own. This drive also has some cool points of interest that add a lot to the tour. The second drive explores eastern San Diego County and has some pretty drastic contrasts. The third takes you up past Willow Springs Raceway and over to Tehachapi, then down to Bakersfield. After that is a three day tour, piggy-backing on the Tehachipi trip and headed for the Gold Country. Lastly are two Death Valley trips. A one (LONG) day trek, and great three day jaunt.

April in Perris-A Really Cheesy Trip

This is maybe not the best tour to do in the summertime. We took several people on this drive a few years ago, and we *baked* in 100+ temps. We called it the "Trains, Planes and Automobiles Tour" because you'll get some of each. One stop is the Orange Empire Railroad Museum in Perris. If you've never been there, you have missed a real gem. If you remember LA with street cars and if you remember the Big Red Cars of the Pacific Electric RR, you'll get a real charge out of this place. If your memories of light rail transit in LA are of the Blue, Gold, and Red Lines, you are in for a shock.

Southern California at one time had the most extensive intercity rail

Ride the Trolleys at the Orange Empire Railway Museum
photo by the author

30

service in the nation. Sadly, following WWII, the system was flat worn out. Add to that the shift to cars and the building of freeways, plus the expense of rebuilding the cars (some of the wooden ones were built in the teens and twenties!) and light rail in SoCal was dead. Some will tell you it was the evil empire of GM, Firestone and the Oil Companies that killed the PE. Not really. They offered a less expensive way to move people: buses. The reality was that Henry Huntington (of Huntington Library fame, and nephew of C. P. Huntington, a founder of the Central Pacific RR of Transcontinental RR fame) built the PE as a way to sell his vast real estate holdings. He provided a way for people in far flung future suburbs to get to LA. Once he made his millions, he sold the line to the Southern Pacific, knowing that cars would take over. The Orange Empire has restored to operating condition several Big Red Cars and well as LA Railway streetcars and they operate them on the weekends. There is no fee to look around, but they charge to ride. It's really worth it though. There is also a very pleasant and shady picnic area so bring a lunch. By the way, there is a surprise along the way that will help you with lunch.

The other museum is at March AFB. Its just up the road from Perris and also worth it. Where else can you get up close and personal with an SR71, a U2, and a B52? There is a fee but also well worth it. March has been an important part of the aerospace history of SoCal and the museum has some excellent exhibits detailing March's place in our local history.

I have to apologize for a bit more freeway on this tour than I'd like. To connect the bits together, it was necessary. We are starting at the usual Denny's in Arcadia. Have breakfast there, but pack a picnic lunch. Some salami and bread will be great, but don't get any cheese. That's available at one of the stops along the way.

A further note: on the weekends, bicyclists love some of these roads. Give 'em a break and share the road.

The Big red Cars still live at OERM
photo by the author

April in Perris-Directions

NORTH on N Santa Anita Ave	0.8 mi
TURN RIGHT to merge onto I-210 E toward San Bernardino	6.5 mi
TAKE EXIT 40 for Azusa Ave/CA-39	0.3 mi
LEFT on Azusa Ave/CA-39 N	1.8 mi
SLIGHT LEFT at N San Gabriel Canyon Rd/CA 39	0.2 mi
Stay on CA 39	10.0 mi
RIGHT on E Fork Rd	5.2 mi
RIGHT on Glendora Mountain Rd	4.9 mi
LEFT on Glendora Ridge Rd	12.0 mi
RIGHT on Mt Baldy Rd	4.7 mi
LEFT on Shinn Rd	102 ft
LEFT stay on Shinn Rd	0.3 mi
CONTINUE SOUTH on N Mountain Ave	2.0 mi
CONTINUE SOUTH on N Euclid Ave	5.3 mi

This is part one. A nice little drive for just an hour or two. To continue, or to only do the cheese and the museums:

LEFT to merge onto I-10 E/San Bernardino Fwy	24.3 mi
EXIT the California St.	0.5 mi
RIGHT on California St	0.2 mi
RIGHT on Redlands Blvd.	75 ft
TAKE 1st LEFT on California St	1.0 mi
LEFT on Barton Rd	0.4 mi
TAKE 2nd RIGHT on San Timoteo Canyon Rd	0.4 mi
TAKE 1st LEFT to stay on San Timoteo Canyon Rd	15.2 mi
RIGHT to merge onto I-10 E toward Banning	1.9 mi
EXIT on CA-79/Beaumont Ave	0.1 mi
RIGHT on Beaumont Ave/CA-79 S	6.0 mi
CONTINUE on Lamb Canyon Rd/N Sanderson Ave	1.9 mi
RIGHT on Ramona Expy	6.9 mi
LEFT on Hansen Ave	2.0 mi
LEFT on Contour Ave	1.1 mi
CONTINUE on Juniper Flats Rd	2.8 mi
RIGHT to stay on Juniper Flats Rd	3.1 mi
LEFT on CA-74 E/Pinacate Rd	2.3 mi
RIGHT on CA-79 S/Winchester Rd	5.0 mi
RIGHT on Holland Rd	0.2 mi

Winchester Cheese Company. 9-5 M-F, 10-4 Sat/Sun. This place make *real* Gouda from their own cows. It is exceptionally good stuff! They have tours available IF they are making cheese that day. Call ahead for a tour (951) 926-4239-or drop in to buy. The OERM has a shady picnic area to ingest your cheesy comestibles!

Road Trippin'

To get to OERM:

LEFT on CA-79 N/Winchester Rd	1.8 mi
LEFT on Patton Ave	2.0 mi
CONTINUE on Domenigoni Pkwy	1.8 mi
CONTINUE on Newport Rd	5.2 mi
RIGHT on Goetz Rd	6.0 mi
LEFT on Mapes Rd	0.6 mi
TAKE 2nd RIGHT onto S a St	
Destination will be on the right	0.2 mi

Orange Empire Railway Museum

2201 South A Street

Perris, CA 92570

To get to the March Base Museum:

NORTH on S. A St toward Alpine Dr	1.6 mi
RIGHT on W 4th St	0.4 mi
TAKE 3rd LEFT onto S D St	0.6 mi
MERGE onto I-215 N via the ramp to Riverside	6.9 mi

You can see the museum from the highway, just follow the signs to the parking.

March Field Air Museum

22550 Van Buren Blvd

March Arb, CA 92518-2400

To head home:

NORTH on I-215 N	203 ft
EXIT on Van Buren Blvd	0.3 mi
LEFT on Van Buren Blvd	367 ft
MERGE onto I-215 S	3.0 mi
EXIT on Ramona Expy/Cajalco Expy	0.2 mi
RIGHT on Cajalco Expy	0.8 mi
CONTINUE on Cajalco Rd	15.9 mi
RIGHT to merge onto I-15 N	4.2 mi
WEST on CA-91 W toward Beach Cities	5.8 mi
SLIGHT RIGHT on CA-71 N/Chino Valley Fwy	
(signs for CA-71/Ontario/Pomona)	17.0 mi
MERGE onto CA-57 N	3.3 mi
WEST I-210 W toward Pasadena	

Eastern San Diego County

So, the question you should be asking about now, is what's to the south of LA? Isn't there anything around San Diego? Well, yes and no. The beach cities on the way to DayGo are great. Good food, especially for breakfast at the 101 Cafe in Encinitas. The problem is traffic. Lots of traffic. Its a nice enough drive if you don't mind traffic. Did I mention the traffic? You can get off the I-5 and follow the old 101 (PCH) from about Long Beach down to about Del Mar, and the beach cities are a lot of fun. There are also neat things to do in San D, but this kind of driving isn't what Road Trips are really about, are they? East of San Diego, all the way to Arizona is a virtually undiscovered country of drastic contrasts. Mountains, forests and empty desert, and that geographical oddity, the Salton Sea are a real treat. Part of this route takes you through the Anza-Borrego Desert. I don't recommend you try this in the summer. Its almost as hot as Death Valley.

Central to this trip is the town of Julian. A bit touristy, but justifiably famous for its Apple Pie. Try "Mom's," the sign outside asks "Do you want *good* pie or *fast* pie?" While it's a good place to stop for a couple of nights while exploring the area if you are alone or with one or two other cars, the accommodations are a bit thin, as are local gas stations. I tagged this trip onto part of the Planes, Trains, Automobiles tour and purposely lead you past the Winchester Cheese Company. No, they don't give me free cheese, I just like the "gouda" stuff!

I also have a confession to make. We haven't yet, as of this writing, driven all of this route, only the parts around Julian. It's on the list, so understand that it is *very* experimental. I have, however, talked to a few folk who are familiar with the area. I trust them. Sort of. So, buckle up, and bring your explorer spirit.

Ready to set off–
photo by Mike Andrews

Road Trippin'

Eastern San Diego County-Day One Directions to Julian

NORTH on Santa Anita Ave	0.8 mi
RIGHT to merge onto I-210 E toward San Bernardino	11.8 mi
CONTINUE on CA-210 E	40.3 mi
EXIT WEST on I-10 W toward Los Angeles	1.3 mi
EXIT on California St	0.3 mi
LEFT on California St	0.3 mi
RIGHT on Redlands Blvd	75 ft
TAKE 1st LEFT on California St (This is a *really* fast right/left!)	1.0 mi
LEFT on Barton Rd	0.4 mi
TAKE 2nd RIGHT on San Timoteo Canyon Rd	0.4 mi
TAKE 1st LEFT to stay on San Timoteo Canyon Rd	15.2 mi
RIGHT to merge onto I-10 E toward Banning	1.9 mi
EXIT on CA-79/Beaumont Ave	0.1 mi
RIGHT on Beaumont Ave/CA-79 S	6.0 mi
CONTINUE on Lamb Canyon Rd/N Sanderson Ave	
Continue to follow N Sanderson Ave	7.2 mi
RIGHT on CA-74 W/CA-79 S/W Florida Ave	4.1 mi
LEFT on CA-79 S/Winchester Rd	3.2 mi

Look for the Winchester Cheese Company at Holland Rd. Great Cheese! It is SOUTH of Domenigoni Pkwy. After you get cheese, Head back NORTH on 79 and go RIGHT on Domenigioni Pkwy.

LEFT (EAST) on Domenigoni Pkwy	7.0 mi
LEFT on S State St	1.8 mi
RIGHT on E Stetson Ave	4.5 mi
LEFT on Fairview Ave	1.2 mi
RIGHT on CA-74 E/Florida Ave	26.5 mi
RIGHT on CA-371 W/Kenworthy Bautista Rd	20.7 mi
RIGHT on CA-79 N	15.3 mi

Look for the Stage Coach Inn. Sunday jam sessions, good blues and burgers!

LEFT on Margarita Rd	52 ft
CONTINUE on Redhawk Pkwy	0.7 mi
RIGHT to stay on Redhawk Pkwy	0.4 mi
TAKE 3rd RIGHT on Wolf Valley Rd	0.9 mi
LEFT on Co Rd 16/Pechanga Pkwy	2.4 mi
CONTINUE on Pala-Temecula Rd	5.0 mi
LEFT on Pala Mission Rd	0.6 mi
CONTINUE on CA-76 E/Pala Rd	6.0 mi
LEFT on Nate Harrison Grade	1.1 mi
LEFT on Nate Harrison Rd	207 ft
CONTINUE on Nate Harrison Grade	489 ft
CONTINUE on Nate Harrison Rd	8.2 mi

Directions continued next page

Eastern San Diego County Continued

CONTINUE on Hwy S7	2.2 mi
CONTINUE on State Park Rd	1.0 mi
RIGHT on S Grade Rd	11.4 mi
LEFT on CA-76 E/Pala Rd	4.5 mi
RIGHT on CA-79 S	7.1 mi
LEFT on CA-78 E/CA-79 S/Julian Rd	
Continue to follow CA-78 E/CA-79 S	6.7 mi
CONTINUE on Washington St	102 ft

230 mi – about 6 hours 12 mins

This is Julian, CA Great places to eat. FABULOUS apple pie!

Eastern San Diego County-Day Two Directions to Yuma and Back

You will need to know where Arizona is today. In fact, you'll need a sense of Yuma. Sorry, I can't help it. I have Pun Tourettets!

HEAD SOUTHWEST on Washington St toward Main St	102 ft
TAKE 1st LEFT on Main St	0.3 mi
CONTINUE on Banner Rd/CA-78 E	3.0 mi
LEFT on Banner-Grade/CA-78 E	15.3 mi
LEFT on Yaqui Pass Rd	7.4 mi
CONTINUE on Rango Way	1.1 mi
CONTINUE on Borrego Valley Rd	2.4 mi
RIGHT on Palm Canyon Dr	2.8 mi
CONTINUE on Pegleg Rd	2.4 mi
CONTINUE on Borrego Salton Sea Way	13.1 mi
CONTINUE on Borrego Salton Sea Way	7.4 mi
RIGHT on CA-86 S (signs for State Hwy 86/)	35.3 mi
CONTINUE on CA-78 E/Main St	7.9 mi
LEFT on Ben Hulse Hwy/CA-78 E	65.2 mi
LEFT on CA-78 E/Rannells Blvd	2.0 mi
RIGHT on 28th Ave/CA-78 E	3.0 mi
LEFT on CA-78 E/S Neighbours Blvd	6.8 mi
TAKE RAMP onto I-10 E	
Entering Arizona	24.6 mi
TAKE EXIT 17 for US-95 toward AZ-95/Yuma/Parker	0.2 mi
LEFT on W Main St/US-95 S	0.2 mi
TAKE 1st RIGHT on W Main St	1.5 mi
This is Quartzsite, AZ	
RIGHT on N Central Blvd/US-95 S	80.2 mi
RIGHT onto the I-8 E ramp	0.3 mi

Directions continued on next page

Eastern San Diego County, Continued

MERGE onto I-8 W

Entering California 14.7 mi

EXIT on Ogilby Rd 24.8 mi

LEFT on Ben Hulse Hwy/CA-78 W 32.4 mi

RIGHT on CA-115 N/CA-78 W 30.6 mi

LEFT to stay on CA-78 W 22.9 mi

RIGHT on Borrego Springs Rd/Borrego Valley Rd 11.5 mi

AT TRAFFIC CIRCLE TAKE 5th EXIT onto Palm Canyon Dr 1.6 mi

LEFT on Co Rd S22/Montezuma Valley Rd 0.7 mi

CONTINUE on Co Hwy S3/Montezuma-Borrego Hwy 9.6 mi

CONTINUE on Montezuma Valley Rd 7.1 mi

RIGHT on San Felipe Rd/San Felipe Valley Rd 4.7 mi

LEFT on CA-79 S 11.4 mi

LEFT on CA-78 E/CA-79 S/Julian Rd 6.7 mi

CONTINUE on Washington St 102 ft

177 mi – about 4 hours 45 mins

Back in Julian, CA

Eastern San Diego County-Day Three Directions-Home

HEAD SOUTHWEST on Washington St toward Main St 0.2 mi

CONTINUE on CA-78 W/CA-79 N/Julian Rd 6.6 mi

RIGHT on CA-79 N 7.1 mi

LEFT on CA-76 W/Pala Rd 27.9 mi

RIGHT on Pala Mission Rd 0.6 mi

RIGHT on Pala-Temecula Rd 5.0 mi

CONTINUE on Co Rd 16/Pala Rd 4.1 mi

LEFT on Temecula Pkwy 0.7 mi

SLIGHT RIGHT to merge onto I-15 N toward Riverside 37.6 mi

EXIT WEST on CA-91 W toward Beach Cities 5.8 mi

SLIGHT RIGHT on CA-71 N/Chino Valley Fwy

(signs for CA-71/Ontario/Pomona) 17.0 mi

MERGE onto CA-57 N 3.3 mi

WEST on I-210 W toward Pasadena

OK, so how was it?

The Donkey Hottie Tour

This trip might be best saved for the spring. It involves a bit of mountain driving and you never know, it might just snow. Angeles Crest in the snow can be, well, exciting in places! Nothing like dirt tracking around a hairpin. Yee HAW! If nothing else, there can be ice up there when it gets cold, especially in the shady spots, and it can linger into the spring. So BE CAREFUL! Another word of caution about Angeles Crest. If you go on a week day, you need to know that there are a bunch of commuters that head over the hill from Palmdale. Some of them move right along, and a few of them cut corners. Again, the CHP *really* patrols the Crest, particularly on weekends when the motorcycle boys are up there playing. The 45 mph speed limit on the part up from La Canada is *absolute*, They hang out in turnouts and can evidently tag you way down the hill with radar and point you in for a ticket when you get there. The other thing they rigidly enforce is the double yellow line. Don't *even* touch it. I'm serious, treat it like a wall. They target the crotch-rocket boys, but us car guys get a look as well. They *know* why we're up there. As for the yellow line, it's pretty scary when some guy is on your side coming at you, so don't do it yourself. If you get behind someone who can't or won't do the 45, hang back and enjoy the scenery. With any luck, he'll pull over at a turn out. If not (which is usual) just be patient, there are a few passing lanes, wait for them. I know I've said all this before, but I can't emphasize these points enough.

Santa Fe Steam Locomotive #3751 at Caliente
photo by the author

38

Road Trippin'

This tour will have a bit of my other passion, trains. Only this time, the real thing on one of the busiest mainlines in the US, and one of the most famous, the Tehachapi Loop. We did this one as a Sunday Drive with a bunch of people a couple of years ago and everyone had a great time. You can either bring a picnic lunch and eat trackside in Caliente, or find one of the eateries in Tehachapi. The Village Inn is good and there is plenty of stuff to see if you wander about the town. I understand they are opening up the old depot as a museum soon, so you might want to check that out. There is also a place in Keane that serves food. For breakfast, I used to recommend the little cafe on Angeles Forest Hwy at Hidden Springs, but sadly, it was lost in the infamous Station Fire of '09. It had been there forever and was a classic mountain roadhouse. When we did this drive a few years ago, we billed it as the Donkey Hottie Tour. It will take you past some of those wind generators up in the Tehachapis and so we named it in honor of that great literary tilter of windmills and an unnamed student of mine who spelled this character's name a bit more phonetically than is normal.

The one downside of this tour is heading home down I-5 and over the Grapevine. Unless you want to head home the same way you came, there really isn't much of an alternate.

The Blue Meanie at speed
photo by Mike Andrews

Donkey Hottie Tour-Tehachapi and Back-Directions

NORTH on N Santa Anita Ave	0.6 mi
RIGHT to merge onto I-210 W to Pasadena Continue on 210 N/W to La Canada	12.0 mi
TAKE the CA-2/Angeles Crest Hwy exit toward La Cañada Flintridge	0.4 mi
RIGHT on Angeles Crest Hwy/CA-2 N	18.1 mi
GO PAST THE ANGELES FOREST HIGHWAY TURN OFF!	
LEFT on Upper Big Tujunga Canyon Rd	9.1 mi
RIGHT on Angeles Forest Hwy/Co Hwy N3	16.2 mi
RIGHT onto Sierra Hwy	0.3 mi
LEFT to merge onto CA-14 N toward Palmdale	4.9 mi
TAKE EXIT 35 for CA-138 E/Palmdale Blvd toward Palmdale	0.3 mi
LEFT on E Palmdale Blvd	1.0 mi
CONTINUE on Elizabeth Lake Rd	16.2 mi
RIGHT on Munz Ranch Rd	4.4 mi
RIGHT on Fairmont-Neenach Rd	0.6 mi
CONTINUE on 120th St W/Lancaster Rd	0.5 mi
LEFT on W Ave I	1.0 mi
TAKE 1st LEFT on 110th St W	5.0 mi
RIGHT on CA-138 E/W Ave D	2.0 mi
LEFT on 90th St W	12.1 mi
LEFT on Tehachapi Willow Springs Rd	14.9 mi
LEFT on E Tehachapi Blvd	4.0 mi

This is Tehachapi

LEFT on Tucker Rd (signs for State Route 202 W)	0.5 mi
TAKE 2nd RIGHT on CA-202 W/Valley Blvd	1.5 mi
RIGHT on Woodford-Tehachapi Rd	9.6 mi
SLIGHT LEFT to stay on Woodford-Tehachapi Rd	0.6 mi
TAKE FIRST LEFT toward CA-58 W	121 ft
RIGHT to merge onto CA-58 W	5.0 mi
RIGHT on Bealville Rd	2.0 mi

This is Caliente-good place for a picnic

LEFT on Caliente Bodfish Rd	4.7 mi
CONTINUE RIGHT on Bena Rd	10.1 mi
CONTINUE on Edison Hwy	4.4 mi
LEFT on S Edison Rd	0.2 mi
RIGHT to merge onto CA-58 W	8.8 mi
EXIT ON LEFT toward CA-99 S/Los Angeles	0.3 mi
KEEP RIGHT at the fork,	
follow signs for CA-99 S/Los Angeles and merge onto CA-99 S	24.5 mi
MERGE onto I-5 S You should be able to find your way back from here!	59.7 mi

There's Gold in Them Thar Hills!

An often overlooked area that needs exploring is the western/southern Sierras. That means, ultimately, the Gold Country. There are a bunch of neat roads and intriguing sights to see, and many of us SoCal folk don't seem to take advantage of the possibilities.

This tour will tag onto the previous one (no sense in reinventing the wheel here) that we called the Donkey Hottie Tour, up to Tehachapi. I've included that tour's beginnings, just to be clear. The first part will take us up over Angeles Crest, then to Willow Springs and the back way to Tehachapi. We'll do some "IFR" driving--"I Follow Railroads"--to Caliente, then the variations.

Part of this tour is *very* seasonally sensitive. The route past Road's End is *closed* during the winter. There is an alternate way out of Lake Isabella, but it involves a *very* tough climb. I've inserted it into the appropriate spot. You will want to call the CHP to find out what roads are open.

Caliente-Bodfish Road, north out the Caliente is a really tricky road that had me in awe of stage coach drivers. Seems back in the days of the Wild West, this was the stage road from Lake Isabella to the railroad station at Caliente. When you drive the road, keep that in mind. Those stage coach guys had *big brass* ones!

Lake Isabella is a very pretty area. Lots of camping and fishing available there. From there, we head north past "Road's End" and to a road that looms large in my own memory. Near the village of Quaking Aspens is a church camp called Quaker Meadows. Back in my youth, to work my way through college, I drove buses for Embree Buses of Pasadena. On a regular basis in the summer, the best of us got the duty of Camp Runs. Big Bear, Running Springs, Osito Rancho and the dreaded Bluff Lake (a couple of fellow drivers with excellent records managed to get *fired* over baloney sandwiches there, of all things) and if you were *really, really* good, you got to do Quaker Meadows. When you take this road, think of me driving a 35' Crown Coach School Bus, loaded with happy kids singing "John Jacob Jingle Heimer Swift" up and down that road. Especially note the one hairpin turn where we all knew we had arrived as *serious* drivers when we could take that turn in one cut, no backing and filling! Of course to do so, the driver's seat was hanging out over *nothing*! Yeah, we had big brass ones too.

The Quaker Meadows Run was also the death of one of our finest buses. Good Ol' 55. It had a SOHC, twin sparkpug/cylinder 590cid Hall-Scott straight six gasoline engine and could do 100 mph. Honest! My buddy Bill took it up to Quaker Meadows, being told by the boss that 20 psi of oil pressure was just fine. The heavy toll on that gallant motor was too much. On the way back, at Mountain Ave. on the 210, that Mighty 590 blew up all over the road. Holed the oil pan, flash oil fire, guts strung along the road, 55 would never haul ass again. (Pause here to wipe away a tear).

The first night will be in Porterville and for once, I won't recommend the Motel 6. A friend checked it out and something about crack labs and "professional ladies" makes it seem a bit sketchy if ya know what I mean. We used the Holiday Inn Express there and the people were great. Ask at the desk for suggestions for eats.

Road Trippin'

The second day of the drive is the gateway to some of the world's natural wonders. Yosemite and includes a sojourn through Sequoia National Park. True gems. We won't try Yosemite on this trip, the road still needs repair, it's always crowded, and really isn't a road trip much as a camp out. If you've never been, shame on you! We will stick with stuff in and around California Highway 49 (get it, 49? As in the '49ers-not not the football team, the guys who took off for Californey in 1849 to get rich in the Mother Lode) and what is generally known as The Gold Country. This can be awfully touristy and in the summer, crowded with motor homes and trailers. Still, there is plenty to see if you get off the main road.

Sometimes, Stuff Happens!
photo by Mike Andrews

First up is the town of Mariposa, an abundance of good eateries in town, and the portal to Yosemite. From there is a side road to the ghost town of Hornitos. I discovered this spot back in those bus driving days of yore. I had a multi-day field trip for a geology class at Pasadena City College that examined the western Sierras as well as some of the historical sites. One was Hornitos. It was named for the several small beehive shaped "ovens" (hornitos in Spanish) that were actually burial sites due to the particularly hard ground. It is also the site of a jail house dating from the 1850s that once lodged none other than the notorious outlaw, Joaquim Murietta. The story is that when Murietta was finally brought to justice, he was executed and his head put in a jar on display in a San Francisco museum of oddities. Gruesome were our forbearers, weren't they?

Another place of interest in the area, if you have time, is Jamestown and the railroad museum there. The Sierra Railroad is a working railway, but is also famous for its steam collection. These steamers have been in almost every Western film for the last 80 years. They still give rides and its worth the side trip.

We're spending the second night in Jackson, one of the centers of mining activity during the Gold Rush. This has a personal connection to your faithful scribe. Go to the old cemetery and look for headstones for Ratto. Yep, great-great-grands of mine. The first of the family to get to California, straight from Italy. I'm a fifth generation Californian, a pretty rare bird indeed. And yes, the family had a gold mine and ranch there. I remember visiting the ranch as a wee lad, as well as the family home in San Francisco that managed to survive the 1906 earthquake. Great Grandpa even had a good friend in San Francisco, named A.P. Giannini. That's a story for another time, however.

We found a gem of a place to eat in Jackson: Teresa's Place. Family run since 1921 and according to my mom, our family used to eat there all the time. What a coincidence. Terrific Italian, I mean *Seriously Terrific*!

On day three, we're taking it easy, using some great back roads to get us to California's own "Mother Road," Highway 99. From there, point yourself south and home.

Aw, how cute! Ya gotta have a mascot!
photo by Marianne McCarthy

Road Trippin'

Gold in Them Thar Hills Directions-Day One-Arcadia to Porterville

HEAD NORTH on N Santa Anita Ave	0.6 mi
RIGHT to merge onto I-210 W toward Pasadena	12.0 mi
Continue N 210 toward La Canada	
TAKE the CA-2/Angeles Crest Hwy exit toward La Cañada Flintridge 0.4 mi	
RIGHT on Angeles Crest Hwy/CA-2 N	9.2 mi
LEFT on Angeles Forest Hwy	24.6 mi
RIGHT on Sierra Hwy	0.3 mi
LEFT to merge onto CA-14 N toward Palmdale	4.9 mi
TAKE EXIT 35 for CA-138 E/Palmdale Blvd. toward Palmdale	0.3 mi
LEFT on E Palmdale Blvd.	1.0 mi
CONTINUE on Elizabeth Lake Rd	15.0 mi
LEFT to stay on Elizabeth Lake Rd	1.2 mi
RIGHT on Munz Ranch Rd	4.4 mi
RIGHT on Fairmont-Neenach Rd	0.6 mi
CONTINUE on 120th St W/Lancaster Rd	0.5 mi
SLIGHT LEFT on W Ave I	1.0 mi
TAKE 1st LEFT on 110th St W	5.0 mi
RIGHT on CA-138 E/W Ave D	2.0 mi
LEFT on 90th St W	12.1 mi
CONTINUE on Tehachapi Willow Springs Rd	14.9 mi
LEFT on E Tehachapi Blvd.	3.0 m

This is Tehachapi, CA. The Village Grill is a good place for lunch. After lunch:

HEAD WEST on W Tehachapi Blvd. toward S Curry St	1.1 mi
LEFT on Tucker Rd (signs for State Route 202 W)	0.5 mi
TAKE 2nd RIGHT on CA-202 W/Valley Blvd.	1.5 mi
RIGHT on Woodford-Tehachapi Rd	9.6 mi
SLIGHT LEFT to stay on Woodford-Tehachapi Rd	0.6 mi
TAKE 1st LEFT toward/CA-58	121 ft
MERGE onto CA-58 W	6.4 mi
LEFT on E Bear Mountain Blvd/CA-223 W	0.2 mi
TAKE 1st RIGHT onto Bena Rd	2.6 mi
SHARP RIGHT on Caliente Bodfish Rd	4.7 mi
LEFT to stay on Caliente Bodfish Rd	0.2 mi
LEFT on Caliente Bodfish Rd	3.0 mi
SLIGHT LEFT on Caliente Creek Rd	19.3 mi
CONTINUE on Walker Basin Rd	6.8 mi
Walker Basin Rd turns right and becomes Johns Rd	0.8 mi
LEFT on Williams Rd	0.5 mi
CONTINUE on Walser Rd	0.5 mi

Directions continue on next page

RIGHT on Caliente Bodfish Rd/Co Rd 483	14.9 mi
CONTINUE on Lake Isabella Blvd.	2.1 mi
RIGHT on Erskine Creek Rd	0.2 mi
TAKE THE 1st LEFT	154 ft
LEFT on Mountain Dr	0.2 mi

This is Lake Isabella, CA

See Below for alternate route if route past Road's end is closed.

HEAD WEST on Mountain Dr toward Lake Ridge Way	0.2 mi
TAKE FIRST RIGHT toward Erskine Creek Rd	154 ft
TAKE 1st RIGHT onto Erskine Creek Rd	0.2 mi
RIGHT on Lake Isabella Blvd.	0.7 mi
TAKE 2nd LEFT on Kernville Rd	0.3 mi
CONTINUE on CA-155 W/Wofford Heights Blvd	6.4 mi
CONTINUE on Burlando Rd/Co Rd 495	4.7 mi
SLIGHT LEFT to stay on Burlando Rd/Co Rd 495	135 ft
LEFT on Co Rd 521/Sierra Way	3.2 mi
CONTINUE on M-99	21.1 mi
M-99 TURNS SLIGHTLY LEFT and becomes M-50/Parker Pass Dr	6.5 mi
RIGHT on M-90	15.4 mi
CONTINUE on CA-190 W	4.1 mi
RIGHT to stay on CA-190 W	2.5 mi
LEFT to stay on CA-190 W	0.1 mi
RIGHT to stay on CA-190 W	2.3 mi
RIGHT to stay on CA-190 W	10.1 mi
LEFT to stay on CA-190 W	21.2 mi
LEFT on S Jaye St	433 ft

Holiday Inn Express Hotel & Suites

ALTERNATE ROUTE!

FROM Lake Isabella Rd:

TAKE 2nd LEFT onto Kernville Rd	0.3 mi
CONTINUE on CA-155 W/Wofford Heights Blvd	6.4 mi
SHARP LEFT on CA-155 W/Evans Rd	6.6 mi
LEFT to stay on CA-155 W/Evans Rd	13.7 mi
RIGHT on White River Rd	1.1 mi
RIGHT on Jack Ranch Rd	4.7 mi
LEFT on Jack Ranch Rd/M-10 Rd	131 ft
Jack Ranch Rd/M-10 Rd turns slightly left and becomes M-3/Old Stage Rd	2.5 mi
CONTINUE on White River Rd	3.5 mi
CONTINUE on Mountain Rd 109	0.4 mi
CONTINUE on Mt Rd 109/Old Stage Rd/Old Stage Coach Rd	18.3 mi

Directions continued on next page

CONTINUE on Rd 264/Holcomb St	0.8 mi
CONTINUE STRAIGHT on Ave 116	1.5 mi
CONTINUE on Rd 252/S Plano St	3.3 mi
LEFT on E Poplar Ave	1.0 mi
LEFT on S Jaye St	

Gold in Them Thar Hills Directions-Day Two-to Jackson, CA

HEAD NORTH on S Jaye St toward Poplar Rd	394 ft
LEFT on W Poplar Ave	0.5 mi
SLIGHT RIGHT onto the State Route 65 N ramp to Lindsay	0.4 mi
MERGE onto CA-65 N	12.2 mi
RIGHT on Rd 204/N Spruce Ave	4.4 mi
CONTINUE on 14th Ave E/S Spruce Rd	
Continue to follow S Spruce Rd	3.5 mi
RIGHT on Ave 296/CA-198 E	25.6 mi
LEFT on CA-198 E/Generals Hwy	5.3 mi
LEFT to stay on CA-198 E/Generals Hwy	39.2 mi
LEFT on CA-180 W/Generals Hwy	22.0 mi
RIGHT on N Elwood Rd	11.8 mi
RIGHT on N Piedra Rd	0.7 mi
RIGHT on E Trimmer Springs Rd	13.7 mi
LEFT on Maxon Rd	5.0 mi
RIGHT on Watts Valley Rd	3.2 mi
CONTINUE on Burrough Valley Rd	3.2 mi
RIGHT to stay on Burrough Valley Rd	1.1 mi
RIGHT on Tollhouse Rd	1.2 mi
CONTINUE on Lodge Rd	6.6 mi
RIGHT on Auberry Rd	2.9 mi
SLIGHT LEFT on Power House Rd	7.4 mi
CONTINUE on Rd 222/Auberry Rd	6.4 mi
LEFT on Rd 200/N Fork Rd	2.9 mi
RIGHT on Rd 221/Crane Valley Rd	194 ft
RIGHT to stay on Rd 221/Crane Valley Rd	1.6 mi
LEFT on Rd 223/Teaford Saddle Rd	6.1 mi
CONTINUE on Rd 426/Crane Valley Rd	6.3 mi
LEFT on CA-41 S	0.3 mi
TAKE 1st RIGHT onto CA-49 N	27.1 mi
LEFT to stay on CA-49 N	36.5 mi
LEFT on CA-120 W/CA-49 N	11.8 mi
RIGHT on CA-108 E/CA-49 N	

This is Jackson, CA

Gold in Them Thar Hills-Directions-Day Three-Home

HEAD SOUTH on CA-49 S/CA-88 E	
Continue to follow CA-49 S	14.6 mi
LEFT on W St Charles St	0.4 mi
TAKE 1st RIGHT on Pool Station Rd	12.6 mi
RIGHT on CA-4 W	4.6 mi
LEFT on Main St	1.4 mi
CONTINUE on O'Byrnes Ferry Rd	6.8 mi
O'Byrnes Ferry Rd TURNS SLIGHTLY RIGHT	
and becomes Co Rd E15/Obyrnes Ferry Rd	4.7 mi
RIGHT on CA-108 W/CA-120 W (signs for Oakdale)	3.2 mi
LEFT on Co Rd J59/La Grange Rd	
Continue to follow La Grange Rd	26.1 mi
LEFT on Co Rd J16/Merced Falls Rd	5.7 mi
RIGHT on Co Rd J16/Hornitos Rd	0.4 mi
SLIGHT RIGHT on Hornitos Rd	7.1 mi
CONTINUE on Bear Valley Rd	0.2 mi

This is Hornitos, CA

HEAD SOUTH on Bear Valley Rd toward Plaza Alley	0.2 mi
SHARP LEFT on Hornitos Rd	12.0 mi
RIGHT on CA-140 E	16.1 mi
LEFT on Plainsburg Rd	7.9 mi
LEFT on CA-99 S	

Its a long trek home on 99, but take your time and cruise.

Even Motorcycles are welcome! Doc Jones on his '44 Indian Chief-only a FEW years ago!
photo by the author

Death Valley Daze

How about somewhere you'd *never* go in the summer? The desert. I'm not talking a trip to Palm Springs, I'm talking *real* desert. Death Valley. No, not a place to go in the summer where the highest recorded temperature in North America was recorded. Would you believe 134 degrees F? That's hot my friends. *exceptionally* hot! Don't think I'll take the TR3 with its typical English "cooling" system there in the summer. Now winter and spring? A whole different deal. The weather can be downright pleasant, the air is wonderfully clear, and the desert scenery is different from anything you've ever seen. The term "moonscape" comes to mind. The idea of crossing this vast expanse on foot or horseback boggles the mind.

Now, one misconception about Death Valley is that it looks like the Sahara. Vast vistas of sand as far as the eye can see. Wrong. The actual area of Death Valley is fairly long and narrow, lying between a couple of mountain ranges. You are actually hemmed in by mountains that are sharp and rugged. No real rainfall to erode the leftovers of Nature heaving itself up against itself. Plenty of evidence that at one time, this was a veritable Hell's Kitchen of volcanic activity.

The other oddity is color. Nope, not just light brown sand. Reds, blacks, whites, and about a hundred shades of browns from near white to chocolate run riot over the landscape, clashing, yet blending in a way to make the most intrepid abstract artist green with envy. In the spring after a rainy winter, it's a riot of other colors from the wildflowers. Proof of life clinging to what one would have thought was a lifeless, God forsaken tract of land.

The route is a long one (about 600 miles) so you may want to break it up into a two day trip. There are some good looking places to stay, the Furnace Creek Inn and resort is probably the nicest and the priciest. There is also a motel at Stovepipe Wells that looked pretty good. Shoshone also has a funky looking motel that could be pretty cool for the nostalgia freaks out there.

Food is also a potential issue. Leave early, say o'Dark-Thirty, and stop for breakfast at the Summit Inn at the top of Cajon Pass. It's been there for ever as part of good old Route 66. We enjoy picnic lunches, and this is a good trip for one. Stop in Olancha for Gus's Really Good Jerky. This stuff is the best jerky I've ever had. Several varieties are available. We like the Cowboy Jerky (mild and great taste) and the Spicy (starts sweet and POW). They have others as well. Add it to your cheese and bread and whatever and you have a pleasant repast. There is also a café/bar in Shoshone. We didn't try it (we were munching jerky) but the place (called the Crowbar) looked busy enough to give it a try.

A couple of other tips. The route takes you over some mountain ranges. These are steep and rugged and twisty. They also seem to go Straight Up and Straight Down, with some *long* straight line bits connecting them. The views are spectacular and the roads over the mountains are challenging. For the one day trip, try to get gas around Ridgecrest, you *do not* want to get gas until you hit Baker on the I-15 if you can avoid it.

The three day trek is designed to stay two nights at the Phoenix/Atomic Inn in Beatty, NV. This is a wonderfully funky place and has a BBQ so you can cook up your own steaks. The people who run it are *great!!* Food in Beatty is limited. The coffee shop in the casino is about the best you'll find. Day Two takes you up to Tonapah and lots of turquoise, then over to 395 and down to Bishop for lunch at a great little BBQ place called Bar BQ Bill's. From there its back across the valley to Beatty. Day Three brings you up to Scotty's Castle (no gas is available there so be careful) and back out the southern end to Baker, then home.

There is a great deal to see in Death Valley and its environs, both natural and man-made. Enjoy it!

Long, Lonely Roads in Death Valley!
Photo by the author

Death Valley Daze-One Long Day Trip-Directions

HEAD NORTH on Santa Anita Ave	0.8 mi
RIGHT to merge onto I-210 E toward San Bernardino	11.8 mi
CONTINUE on CA 210 E	18.2 mi
EXIT onto I-15 N toward Barstow	24.6 mi
SLIGHT RIGHT on US-395 N	
(signs for US-395/Bishop/Adelanto)	98.3 mi
TAKE RAMP onto Three Flags Hwy/US-395	42.0 mi
RIGHT on CA-190 E	14.6 mi
RIGHT to stay on CA-190 E	61.1 mi

272 mi – about 6 hours 16 mins

This is Stovepipe Wells

CONTINUE EAST on CA-190 E	55.2 mi
RIGHT on CA-127 S	27.2 mi

82.4 mi – about 2 hours 5 mins

This is Shoshone, CA

CONTINUE SOUTH on CA-127 S/CA-178 E toward CA-178 E	56.2 mi
RIGHT to merge onto I-15 S	129 mi
EXIT onto CA-210 W toward Pasadena	

219 mi – about 3 hours 58 mins

Marianne at Sea Level-Stovepipe Wells, Death Valley
photo by the author

Death Valley Daze-Directions for the Three Day Monster Trip

NORTH on N Santa Anita Ave	0.5 mi
RIGHT on the US-210 ramp to SAN BERNARDINO	0.2 mi
MERGE onto I-210 E	30.6 mi
EXIT onto I-15 N toward BARSTOW	10.0 mi
TAKE EXIT 124 for Kenwood Ave	0.3 mi
LEFT on Kenwood Ave/US-66	0.2 mi
TAKE 2nd RIGHT on Cajon Blvd/US-66	6.4 mi
LEFT to merge onto I-15 N	1.0 mi
EXIT on CA-138 exit toward Palmdale	0.3 mi
RIGHT on CA-138	2.6 mi
RIGHT to stay on CA-138	5.7 mi
LEFT on CA-173	7.0 mi
LEFT on Arrowhead Lake Rd	5.7 mi
RIGHT on Rocksprings Rd	2.8 mi
LEFT on Kiowa Rd	3.5 mi
RIGHT on Bear Valley Rd	4.7 mi
RIGHT on CA-18/US-18	10.6 mi
CONTINUE STRAIGHT on CA-18/Old Woman Springs Rd	0.3 mi
LEFT on Barstow Rd/CA-247	33.9 mi
RIGHT/EAST at E Main St	

This is Barstow! Several Stations are on Main Street. After Gassing up, head BACK (WEST) on Main the way you came Then:

RIGHT on N 1st Ave

Lunch Stop on the right before the bridge. This is the ORIGINAL Del Taco! Buy to go and eat at the Museum/Train Station. Cross the bridge over the tracks.

Barstow Route 66 "Mother Road" Museum

681 N. First Avenue

will be on the right across the bridge	0.6 mi

127 mi – about 2 hours 43 mins

This is a really cool museum. The people are very nice. The train station is the restored Harvey House--El Desierito. Stop and look around!

After Lunch:

Out of parking lot, turn RIGHT on N 1st Ave.	0.3 mi
TAKE 1st LEFT on Irwin Rd	0.5 mi
TAKE 3rd LEFT on CA-466/Old Hwy 58/US-58	5.9 mi
LEFT on Lenwood Rd	0.4 mi
RIGHT on CA-58	25.1 mi
RIGHT on US-395	35.7 mi

Directions continue on next page

RIGHT on Searles Station Rd/Searles Station Cutoff	6.3 mi
LEFT on Trona Rd	8.5 mi
RIGHT on CA-178/Trona Rd	14.4 mi
CONTINUE to follow CA-178BecomesTrona/Wildrose Rd.	40.7 mi

35. Sharp left at CA-178/Panamint Valley Rd

You can go straight on Wildrose, the road is rough at first, but a lot of fun!

You get back to 190	21.1 mi

There is GAS at Stovepipe Wells After you turn onto CA 190 but it ain't cheap!

RIGHT on CA-178/CA-190	16.4 mi
LEFT on North Hwy	0.6 mi

RIGHT on Daylight Pass Rd This comes up really quick so watch for it!

Remember, you are heading to Beatty, Nevada	13.2 mi
CONTINUE on NV-374	12.8 mi
CONTINUE on W Main St/US-95	0.3 mi

RIGHT on First St.

This is Beatty, NV

105 mi – about 3 hours 13 mins

Death Valley Daze-Directions Day Two

HEAD NORTHWEST on S 1st St toward Watson St	0.1 mi

TAKE 2nd RIGHT on E Main St/US-95

HEAD NORTHEAST on E Hwy-95 N/US-95

GAS UP IN TONOPAH! Yeah, its only been 100 miles or so, but DO IT!

Gentlemen: Keep an eye on the Ladies and your Wallets! Tonapah has TURQUOISE!

Continue to follow US-95	133 mi
LEFT on US-6	22.1 mi

155 mi – about 2 hours 52 mins

Basalt, Mineral, Nevada

And yeah, ya might want to Gas up AGAIN! Better safe than sorry.

HEAD SOUTHWEST on US-6

Entering California	52.4 mi

LEFT on N Main St

BBQ Bill's for Lunch!

Destination will be on the right	0.9 mi

187 S Main St

Bishop, CA Gas up here again!

HEAD SOUTH on CA-168/S Main St/US-395 toward Short St	14.5 mi

LEFT on CA-168 Careful, this gets a bit steep!

Entering Nevada	42.1 mi
RIGHT on NV-266	40.1 mi
RIGHT on US-95	51.4 mi

LEFT on First St.

Back in Beatty, NV 148 mi – about 3 hours 19 mins

End of Day Two

Death Valley Daze-Directions Day Three

HEAD NORTHWEST on S 1st St toward Watson St	0.1 mi
TAKE 2nd RIGHT on E Main St/US-95	35.4 mi
LEFT on NV-267/Sutton	
Entering California	21.5 mi
CONTINUE on North Hwy	4.6 mi
RIGHT into **Scotty's Castle**	0.1 mi

61.7 mi – about 1 hour 20 mins
Scottie's Castle is one of the Wonders of Death Valley.
 Its worth a look around. Take the tour.
There is NO GAS At Scotty's Castle!

HEAD SOUTHWEST toward N Hwy	0.1 mi
RIGHT on North Hwy	36.3 mi

A right turn onto 190 will lead you to Stovepipe Wells and gas,
its a bit closer than Furnace Creek.

LEFT on North Hwy/CA-178/CA-190	18.4 mi

54.8 mi – about 1 hour 24 mins

Furnace Creek, CA

HEAD SOUTHWEST on Badwater Rd/CA-178 toward Death Valley National Park Continue to follow CA-178	70.7 mi
RIGHT on CA-127/CA-178	1.7 mi

72.4 mi – about 2 hours 25 mins
Lunch Stop at the Crow Bar in Shoshone!

Shoshone, CA
There is Gas in Shoshone! Next Gas is in Baker!

HEAD SOUTH on CA-127	56.2 mi
RIGHT to merge onto I-15 S toward BARSTOW	66.0 mi
EXIT on CA-58 toward Bakersfield	1.2 mi
EXIT on W Main St	0.2 mi
LEFT on Main St/US-66	1.0 mi
HEAD SOUTHWEST on Main St/National Trails Hwy/US-66 toward Ash Rd	20.9 mi

This is the original Route 66. Get your kicks on the way home.
Its more fun than the Interstate!

CONTINUE on National Trails Hwy/US-66	26.9 mi
HEAD SOUTHWEST on National Trails Hwy/US-66 toward Private Rd	4.3 mi
TAKE RAMP onto CA-18 W/I-15 S	27.6 mi
EXIT onto I-15 S toward San Diego/Los Angeles	8.0 mi
TAKE CA-210 exit toward Pasadena	

Outside of California Trips

Yeah, there *are* roads outside of California. Spectacular roads. Incredible scenery. Funky places to stay and see. Everything that road trips are about. Washington state, Arizona, New Mexico and a bit of Utah and Colorado are on the menu for this part of the book. So hang on and enjoy the drives. The Roue 66 trip is pretty easy to follow, and the story gives you an idea of where to go. The Great Arizona/New Mexico Turquoise Trek is a bit more complex, but well worth the four days it took us. The Pacific Northwest jaunt is an even larger undertaking, as it will take a couple of days to get up there and a couple of days returning. You will want to spend a good week at least while there, so it fits with a nice two week vacation. Do they still have those?

Route 66, the Mother Road

"If you ever plan to motor west/ take the highway that's the byway that's the best/ Get your Kicks, on Route 66…" A couple of years ago, we gave in to the lure of the "Mother Road" and what book on Road Trips would miss an opportunity to give some impressions and tips on how to get your kicks. Route 66 has been marketed into legend status by nostalgia buffs (and local municipalities hoping to capitalize on the hype) longing for the lure of the open road and the good ol'' days. Now I could get all cynical and tell you its a bunch of bull and that the ol' days weren't much good, that it's only the rosy afterglow of fond memories that ignore the reality, but I'm not gonna do it. We had a great time exploring the longest stretch of the original highway available. In addition, we managed to include a side trip to the Grand Canyon, via the Grand Canyon Railway. The people were friendly, the scenery at times indescribably spectacular, the tourist traps as funky as ever, and we let that rosy glow envelope us like a warm quilt on a cold rainy day.

I probably don't need to go too much into the background of what is referred to as America's Main Street to you fellow road warriors, but here are a few basics. Route 66 was the first paved transcontinental highway. It got its designation in 1926 when it was little more than a dirt wagon trail that paralleled the Santa Fe Railroad from Chicago to Los Angeles, about 2500 miles. Paving wasn't complete until the 1930s, when it became the main route for escapees from the Dust Bowl during the depression. It connected towns that were water and fuel stops along the railroad. As the road was more traveled, wide spots in the road sprang up to provide travelers with places to stay, food and services for their cars. The highway became the main street of the town and those lucky enough to be a day's drive from the last stop became more prosperous, the others scraped by, trying to lure weary travelers with promises of local delights (SEE THE WORLD'S LARGEST BALL OF TWINE! SEE A GENUINE JACK-A-LOPE!) What today is hardest to comprehend is that the whole thing was a *two lane road* and dangerous as all get out! Do any of you realize that along the California stretch from Needles westward, the nearest hospital was in San Bernardino? When news of an accident reached Barstow, the local coroner went with the ambulance and wrecker. No paramedics, no mercy airlifts, just a battered Cadillac Meat Wagon and a tow truck.

Road Trippin'

But enough of then, let's talk about now. Head east on the 210, then the 15 north towards Barstow. To get started on 66, exit at Kenwood (the first exit as the 15 and 215 merge), turn left, then right at the end. This is old 66. As the road bends to the right at Blue Cut, you pass a rest area on the left. This is "Okie Flats," a camp spot for Dust Bowl migrants. The road bends back to the left and towards the end, passes what was Cajon Station on the Santa Fe RR. Get back on the freeway and continue north on I-15. The drive up Cajon Pass obliterated the old road, but at the top, look for the Summit Inn on the right. It's a pretty decent cafe that is an original Route 66 stop. You can eat there but it was early yet for us and we planned a stop in Barstow. In Victorville, we got off at D Street and turned left. This is more of old 66 and will take you through Oro Grande, and Helendale before arriving in Barstow. This is a road of broken dreams, abandoned gas stations and motels, bypassed by the interstate. Like it always did, 66 takes you through the center of Barstow. Note the El Rancho Motel. It was built in 1944 completely of old railroad ties. Also a left turn at the El Rancho (onto First St.) will take you to the Barstow station and the restored Harvey House, El Desierto. There are also neat railroad and Route 66 museum/gift shops there. This makes a nice day trip on it's own. We ate at Denny's in Barstow, then we gassed up. Why so early on a gas stop? Barstow gas prices are reasonable. If you wait for Needles, you will get *gouged*--80 cents a gallon more!

We changed drivers at this point and stayed on the I-40 to Needles. You can exit for Dagget and continue on 66 through Amboy to Needles, but we wanted to make a bit more time. Arizona was where we wanted to get to. Besides, most of 66 along this route runs right along I-40 and the road is *very* rough. Dagget, Newberry Springs (the Bagdad Cafe of movie fame), Ludlow, and Amboy are worth checking out though. In Needles we changed drivers again and were ready for our assault on the road to Oatman.

Just over the Colorado River, we exited at Golden Shores. This is part of the original alignment of 66 and the road to Oatman is a challenge. Evidently, in the old days, travelers would hire locals to drive them over the mountain pass. Brakes and handling from the 1930s or even 50s must have made for a real E Ticket Ride. This road is twisty and the turns aren't all that well marked. BE CAREFUL! Ask me in private and I'll tell you how I know. It's easy to understand why this road was one of the first bypassed by a better highway from Needles to Kingman.

Oatman is a hoot! It's an old mining town that is now a tourist spot. Stop and look around and if you time things right, every day at High Noon (their time, remember, Arizona is Mountain Standard Time and they don't do Daylight Savings in the summer) the Oatman Outlaws stage a gun fight on the main (well, the only) street. It's a bunch of fun and they raise money for charity. The shops area blend of happy crappy and nice jewelry. A herd of wild burros roam the town as well. After Oatman, the road *really* gets twisty and steep. Take it easy. Look for Cool Springs after you crest the summit. It's an old stone gas station that's been restored to a museum and gift shop. Its worth a stop. Good prices on locally made Indian jewelry.

High Noon in Oatman
photo by the author

After this, the road straightens out for the leg to Kingman. Kingman has a lot to offer. There are plenty of old motels but to us, the highlight is Mr. Dz Diner. The place dates to the 1920s but is now a 50s style diner. The food is really good, basic burger fare, the staff is friendly and it makes a good place to stop for lunch. Across the street, check the steam engine on display. Across the highway (Andy Devine St. of all things) is a very good Route 66 museum and (of course) gift shop. After a look around, we headed out of town east, staying on 66. Kingman has grown a lot since the 60s so it will take a bit before you are on the road again.

Broken Dreams on Old 66
photo by Brianna McCarthy

Once out of Kingman, the magic really sets in. This is really the mother road. Two-lane blacktop that stretches to the horizon. Spectacular scenery of eroded sandstone cliffs, and HEY, what's this? A red sign with white letters "Slow Down Pa." is all it says. Hey, another "Sakes Alive!". Nah, it couldn't be! "Ma Just Missed." No *really*? "Signs 4 and 5!" YES!!! "BURMA SHAVE!" OMIGOD! We've hit a time warp. There are about a half dozen brand new metal Burma Shave Signs on each side of the highway. How totally cool is that? I have to give Arizona full praise for promoting the Route 66 Experience.

After rolling through Peach Springs, slowing down for the small town speed trap, we resisted the temptation of the Grand Canyon Caverns on this trip. Its a classic tourist stop. There's a motel on the highway and along a side road is a cafe and entrance to the caverns. Finally we rolled into Seligman for the night. There are several places to stay here. Two are AAA approved. The "Historic Route 66 Motel" looks good and has a history. It used to be the "Navajo Motel" and is a classic Route 66 motel. We opted for the slightly more funky "Deluxe Route 66 Motel." It is also a classic of the type. It may look a bit chancy but it really is a neat place. The rooms are comfortable and clean. The heater was a bit noisy and the train tracks run about 50' from the motel, but hey, we wanted the real experience. The young man who ran things was very helpful and pleasant and I'm sorry that we didn't get his name. He runs a nice place. He recommended an eatery up the street and told us that we could get a 10% discount for staying in his place. This eatery is really fun. It's called "The Road Kill Cafe." They play up the whole road kill idea with menu items like "Fender Tenders" and "Ground Round Hound." They even have a kosher menu--anything hit by a Cadillac. We had really good steaks and garlic scampi. The staff were outstanding and friendly. And yes, I bought a t-shirt. After a few beers, and fully sated, we rolled back to the Deluxe for a restful night's sleep, lulled to sleep by the pounding of the incessant trains rumbling by throughout the night.

We got up the next morning at 6 AM and a snow storm. We had seen evidence of snow and had watched the weather channel, so we were not surprised. We packed up and were off to Williams for our next adventure. We got onto I-40 as soon as possible, thinking (rightly) that the interstate would be kept clear. We rolled into Williams about 7 AM and up to the Grand Canyon Railway Hotel. The snow was getting worse and we were glad we had planned this side trip. Since January is the off season, we were able to check into our room early. Wow, what a change from the friendly Deluxe. A proper hotel with all the amenities. It was a neat contrast to see what an extra $100 (or more) a night will get you. The GCRR Hotel is an extremely comfortable, modern place but designed to have the warmth and feel of a much older hotel. There was a roaring fire in the lobby's fireplace, and a great bar with nineteenth century decor. The staff is what you would expect: friendly, helpful and efficient. Triple A gives it a 3 Gem Rating and they are right. This is a wonderful place. After getting our bags to the room, there was time for breakfast at Max and Thelma's, the hotel's restaurant. They have a buffet as well as a menu. Both are good. The pancakes with strawberries were excellent and the real sausages were big and juicy.

The whole point of this stop in Williams (it's only 40 miles from Seligman) was the train. The Grand Canyon Railroad offers package deals for a night's stay, dinner and breakfast, and a train ride to stay, dinner and breakfast, and a train ride to the Grand Canyon. These are very good deals. There are several levels of comfort from coach (a good deal for families) to luxury. The luxury observation car or the dome car are worth the extra money. In the summer, they trot out their steam engine and that makes it a real train ride! The station is right across the courtyard from the hotel so everything is very convenient. We got our tickets and waited in the station to board. By this time the snow was coming down hard and we were glad that driving to the canyon was not something we would have to do.

The train ride takes about 2 ½ hours and winds through desert scrub and pinon pines and eventually ponderosa pine forests. The ride is relaxing and makes you wonder why anyone takes a plane! Even in coach, the seats have leg room. I'm 6'1" and needed the foot rest. Poor Marianne couldn't reach the seat in front of us. In addition, there is a full bar on board and each car has an attendant (Victoria was a gem!) who will be glad to serve you. An entertainer also comes along to play and sing and generally laugh it up. Its a great time. We got up to the Canyon station (the only operating log constructed train station in the nation) about noon and the snow was still coming down. Huffing and puffing up the walkway (the Grand Canyon rim is at 7800' elevation!), we got to the rim to find the canyon full of clouds. We wandered into a couple of stores, the Hopi House was the best, and Marianne fulfilled part of her Turquoise Quest with pair of earrings. Things eventually started to clear up and we were able to see the Canyon. All I can say is "WOW!" The whole thing looks unreal. It's surely a painted backdrop. Nature's color palette is astounding. Reds, greens, five hundred shades of brown, stacked like a layer cake gone mad. It's also *huge*! A mile down to the bottom and 18 miles across. "Grand" is too puny a word but what else can you call it. By this time we were freezing and opted for a light lunch at the El Tovar Hotel. Exceptionally good French Onion Soup and bread. What else do you need? The train left at 3:30 *sharp* and we were in the observation car. This was the end car and had the classic platform so taking pictures was a great lot of fun. The snow eased up some about halfway back to Williams and we spotted a herd of elk off to the side. Arrival in Williams was about 6 PM, so we went back to our room, pulled off several layers and went back to Max and Thelma's for dinner. A good buffet with prime rib was laid on. Try the local beers, they are very good.

After a more restful night than Seligman, we shoveled off the

The only operating log RR station in the country
photo by the author

57

car (by the way, we took the Mustang, *not* the TR3-we may be crazy but not stupid).

This was a new experience for this SoCal boy. Following a brief snowball fight, we were off to breakfast in Flagstaff. We took a turn through Williams itself and spotted what looked like a number of good places. Had we time and better weather, we would have liked to explore the town more. In Flagstaff, we found a place called, "The Place." Its a great local diner, just on the western outskirts of the older part of town, south of the tracks. Fueled up with waffles, we headed south to Sedona.

Serendipity struck as we left the interstate and headed for the canyon road to Sedona. Out of Flagstaff, head south on I-17 but exit for Hwy 89A to Sedona. Look for Oak Creek Canyon National Park. There is not only a great view and hiking trails, but we discovered an outdoor market. Navajo ladies were just setting up, shoveling snow off the tables and selling jewelry. Marianne was in heaven. Good prices and all locally made, it's fun to hear that the seller's cousin or husband or they themselves made the wares on display.

Having bought a ring, we were off on the road again, looking for Sedona. There is more amazing scenery along the way. Take your time and have a camera ready. We rolled into Sedona about lunch time and opted for some local buffalo jerky and trial mix, rather than a sit down meal. We wandered through shops (Sedona is more than a bit Yuppified, sorry to say, and the New Age Energy Focal Points are a bit much for me) and resisted the lure of a jeep tour through the surrounding landscape. The rock formations are incredible red monoliths that light up in the sun. They've also

We love the Blue Meanie, but the 'Stang is sometimes more...appropriate!
photo by Marianne McCarthy

been in dozens of movies, and for good reason. After Sedona, it was on the Phoenix and home on the 10. This last bit is not a great dive. It just gets you home.

Northern Arizona surprised us with the variety of scenery, the good eats, the nice people and the nostalgic rosy haze that enveloped the whole trip. Take some time and explore. Buy into the legend and enjoy. Get some kicks on Route 66!

Arizona and Route 66 Directions

EAST on I-210 E toward San Bernardino	30.0 mi
NORTH on I-15 N toward Barstow	10.0 mi
TAKE EXIT 124 for Kenwood Ave	0.2 mi
LEFT on Kenwood Ave	0.2 mi
RIGHT on Cajon Blvd	6.4 mi
LEFT to merge onto I-15 N toward Victorville	21.2 mi
EXIT on D St/CA-18	0.4 mi
LEFT on D St	37.6 mi
MERGE onto I-40 E via the ramp to Needles	154 mi
TAKE EXIT 1 toward Golden Shores 1/Oatman	0.2 mi
LEFT on Co Hwy 10/Oatman-Topock Hwy	
Continue to follow Oatman-Topock Hwy	28.4 mi
Oatman-Topock Hwy TURNS SLIGHTLY LEFT	
and becomes Co Hwy 10	19.4 mi
RIGHT on Historic U.S. 66 E	0.4 mi
LEFT to merge onto I-40 E toward Flagstaff	8.5 mi
TAKE EXIT 53 for State Route 66 E/Andy Devine Ave	
toward Kingman Airport	0.2 mi
LEFT on 93 S/E Andy Devine Ave/AZ-66 E/B-I 40	
Continue to follow AZ-66 E	86.4 mi
LEFT to merge onto I-40 E toward Flagstaff	71.8 mi
TAKE EXIT 195 to merge onto I-17 S	
toward Arizona 89A S/Phoenix	2.5 mi
TAKE EXIT 337 toward Arizona 89A S	
/Oak Creek Canyon/Sedona	0.3 mi
RIGHT toward Arizona 89A S	121 ft
LEFT on Arizona 89A S	24.3 mi
LEFT on AZ-179 S	0.4 mi
RIGHT to stay on AZ-179 S	
Continue on AZ-179-S	14.1 mi
RIGHT to merge onto I-17 S toward Phoenix	83.0 mi
TAKE EXIT 214C to merge onto AZ-101 Loop W	22.0 mi
TAKE EXIT 1-A to merge onto I-10 W toward Los Angeles	334 mi

From here, the rest is obvious! Keep on the I-10 until you get to where you started from.

The Great Arizona/New Mexico Turquoise Trek

The director John Ford was a master of portraying the Wild West. His panoramic shots of lonely monoliths in the vast expanse of the desert set the standard for cinematic excellence. Whether it's "Stagecoach," "She Wore a Yellow Ribbon," or "Fort Apache," his camera work gave us city folk a feel for the wide, empty spaces and the diminutive nature of man when pitted against such a back drop. So what does this have to do with Road Trips? Everything.

One January, Marianne and I mounted our trusty Mustang and headed to Indian Country. OK, "Native American Country." Northeast Arizona, a bit of Utah, Northwest New Mexico, and a dab of Colorado. Four days and 2000 miles of the most spectacular back country imaginable. Monument Valley, Shiprock, Chama, Taos, Santa Fe, Gallup, Petrified Forest, Apache, Navajo, Hopi, and Zuni Country. Turquoise by the bucket full, honest-to-God Dinosaur tracks, and narrow gauge railroading, all connected by some high speed driving. What's not to love?

We started at the now obligatory Butt Crack o'Dawn, and headed for breakfast in Barstow. Just wanting to make tracks, we stayed on I-15 to Barstow and found our favorite Denny's for the usual Grand Slam Breakfast. You can always count on Denny's for a decent order of pancakes and the place in Barstow has classical music playing. Nice and soothing in the early morning hours. As usual, we filled up in Barstow to avoid spending the extra eighty cents a gallon in Needles.

As a precaution after a few close calls on the last couple of trips, I borrowed a buddy's Escort Passport Radar Detector. Not that we were planning on hyper speeds, but ya never know if Smokey got up on the wrong side of the bed and is writing for 72 mph. Damn, but that thing works. It reads X, K, Ka, Laser, and Pop Up and gives you *plenty* of time to back off. Like several *miles* of lead time. A real worthwhile investment.

We did stop in Needles to pee and swap drivers, then on to Kingman and old 66. Yeah, we've done it before, but it is a very pleasant stretch of road. We made excellent time and actually got to Williams waaay earlier than we thought we would. In Williams we shunned the luxury of the Grand Canyon Railroad Hotel for the more modest (and decidedly funky) digs of the "9 Arizona Motel" right on the main drag of Williams. For $35 we were ushered into the Marilyn Monroe Suite, no less. Well, heck, there *were* posters of dear Norma Jean on the walls. Talk about *Klass*. It was comfortable and warm and clean, so who can complain? Last trip there, we didn't have time to explore Williams, so we set out to walk the town and find lunch. A word of advice: Don't go to Williams on a Monday. The place shuts down. A few touristy shops were open and Marianne found some turquoise at one, but since most of the town thrives on tourists on the weekends, Mondays are the semi-official day of rest for most. Another word of advice: Don't eat at the Pine Country Cafe. A local merchant recommended it and it was *really bad*. My burger had grease on the *outside* of the bun. BLEEECH! At least they took it off the bill. For dinner, we wanted to try what looked like a great BBQ place, but it was closed (Monday, remember?) and settled on a 50s Cruisin' Joint (called appropriately "Cruisers"), all duded up with car stuff (the privacy wall in the restroom was a pair of pick up truck tailgates, and the divider between the urinal and the sink was a VW bus door. Points for creativity). The food (sizzling steak and 'shrooms with Jack Daniel's Sauce) was quite tasty.

The next day, we got up early again and headed to Flagstaff on I-40 for breakfast at "The Place," a proper eatery with great breakfast that we discovered last year. After breakfast, we started the meat of the trip. Just out of Flagstaff, head north on US 89. This will take you into the heart of the Navajo and Hopi Reservations, and what may be the most spectacular scenery on God's green (well, reddish brown, in this case to be honest) Earth. Gas up in either Williams or Flagstaff because chances will be few and far between.

First stop of interest is the Cameron Trading Post. Its located on the Little Colorado River Gorge and lemme tell ya, HIDE THE CHECK BOOK! CUT UP THE CREDIT CARDS! This place, open since the late 1800s is the Mother Lode for turquoise jewelry. Marianne was *stunned* when she walked in. By now you may have gathered that she is a Certified Turquoise Freak, having collected jewelry since she was about fourteen. She planned ahead on this trip and was wearing her best stuff. This became a key strategic move on her part, as it established herself as a Serious Turquoise Aficionado. People were always asking to see her stuff closer, which led to long conversations and frequently, discounts. SCORE! Any-who, she grazed from case to case, oohing and aaahhhing and got the attention of a lovely lady on the sales staff. Here's a tip, by the way, for the would-be buyer: Look for "Dead Pawn." This is the really old and exceptionally good stuff that was picked up for a song in pawn shops all around the state. The prices are decent and the quality (types of turquoise no longer available and "old" silver--typically from melted down coins from when our small change was really silver) is outstanding. This stuff has a weight and a patina that can't be duplicated today. Marianne finally settled for an older silver hummingbird pin and a pair of very old earrings. When I *finally* dragged her out, I *swear* she was trying to trade the *car* for more stuff.

We continued driving north on 89 to the town of Tuba City, no, really, Tuba City, and ran into our next serendipitous find. In Tuba City, turn right on US 160 and you'll see some really crude signs on scrap plywood announcing "Dinosaur Tracks!" Yeah, we were thinking the same as you. Sure enough, a few miles out of town, the big sign said, "Dinosaur Tracks Here" and pointed up a dirt road. We bit. We had to. About 100 yards up the dirt road was a collections of ramshackle stands. Kinda like roadside fruit stands, but looking like they were a hundred years old and about to fall down. These stands sell locally made jewelry. They are all over the place and some serious bargains can be had. Next to one of them was a crude sign: "Park Here For Dinosaur Tracks." OK, we parked. Up comes this young Navajo man in a parka (this was January, mind you, and it had snowed the week before) and we asked him what the deal was.

"Its a donation. Pay what you feel is OK." What do you say to this? I asked for the $5 each tour and gave him the dough. What's to lose? It was worth it. He led us out for about 200 yards around what was an ancient river bed. In his hand was a gallon jug of water that

Dino Tracks! REALLY!
photo by Marianne McCarthy

he splashed into Honest-To-God-No-Foolin' Dinosaur tracks, frozen in time from millennia ago. You could easily tell that the critters had actually walked there. On top of that, there were places with *bones*. OMIGOD! Real dinosaur BONES, sticking out of the ground. Sadly, our guide told us that the best examples had been cut out in the 40s and 50s and are in museums and private collections, but what is there, however, is still worth the stop.

Back on the road again looking for US Highway 163 in the town of Kayenta, the entrance to Monument Valley. This is where all those John Ford westerns (and countless others) were filmed. We were struck dumb. First, it is impossible with mere pictures to convey the scale of these volcanic monoliths. They are *huge*, jutting up from the desert floor like a giant's rotting teeth. They are also much closer together than you might think. We had to stop every few hundred yards to drink it all in and take pictures. We also had to stop (big surprise) at more jewelry stands. Its a 60 mile or so side trip that is well worth it. Each formation has a name and there is tourist information available in Kayenta with all the details. Kayenta also has some motels if you want to spend more time there to explore. I'm telling ya, this should be on *everyone's* "List of Stuff To Do/See Before Ya Die!" Pictures and words, no matter how skillfully presented cannot possibly convey the scale, majesty, and overwhelming nature of this slice of Arizona and Utah. Uh, did I say Utah?

Denver & Rio Grande Narrow Gauge Steam!
photo by the author

Well, as a matter of fact, yes. Highway 163 crosses over into Utah and the valley does not seem to respect sate boundaries. Imagine *that!* Just before the junction of Route 261 is Mexican Hat. More of a sombrero rock formation than a town, but both are neat. Continue on 163 towards Bluff, but turn south (right) on 191. This will take you back to US 160 at Mexican Water. We found lunch and gas (not mutually related, the food was good) in a diner in Mexican Water. Sadly, we didn't write down the name of the place. Sorry about that. Any way, continue east on 160 towards the New Mexico Border at Tec Nos Pos. We took US 64 east at Tec Nos Pos into New Mexico towards Shiprock. If you thought the other formations were something, wait till ya see *this* one.

Shiprock looks like, well, a sailboat. A really *big* sailboat. Sailing on a flat desert sea with *nothing* around it for miles. A sailboat with a mast that peaks at 7,178 feet. Damn thing must be at least 2000 feet above the desert floor. When the light is right, and the day hot enough, the mirage effect completes the illusion and it actually floats on the shimmering "sea." I mean, DAMN!

Just past Shiprock, are the towns of Farmington and Bloomfield. Honestly, not much to recommend them for, at least what we saw of them. If you have time, head north on 516 to Aztec Ruins National Monument. We didn't but have heard good things about it. We stayed on 64 east towards Chama and a bed for the night. After Bloomfield, the road goes through the southern edge of the Rockies and is a really neat road. Lots of high speed sweepers and enough twisty bits to keep it interesting. Traffic was light, so we could roll right along. So there we are, moving, but not *hauling* and this damn pick up truck, *pulling* a freaking trailer *with* an International Scout loaded on it is catching us. So, not wanting to have to follow a truck with a trailer, I step it up. And he's still there. So, I step it up some more. I'm starting to really haul the mail as they say, and in the twisty bits, I can pull away, but he's willing to hammer it on the straights and mostly straight bits and keeps up. Damn local road knowledge. By the way, do you remember that this was *January* when we took the trip? These are the mountains and there is plenty of snow, and by the way, plenty of shady areas where one might expect *ice*? Had to be *really* careful of my driving line. He finally got stuck behind a slower car I got the chance to pass just before the town of Dulce, but it was a quite nice bit of high speed driving for a good 50 miles.

We rolled into Chama as it was getting dark and found very good (if a bit more expensive than Williams) lodging at the Chama Trails Inn. We really enjoyed the place. Neat, clean, and the owner, Chester Maez is a real character.

"How much for a night?"

"Oh, about $600, but that includes the spa."

"HUH?"

"No, son, just pullin' yer leg. We don't got a spa!"

He *did* put us on to the best food of the trip (so far). The High Country Inn Bar/Resturant is exceptional. Cornbreaded trout (local and fresh, of course) and a mushroom soup that was to *die* for. Not the sticky mucilage you get out of that red and white can, but more like pureed 'shrooms, redolent of the earth. "Rich" doesn't do the flavor justice. One of the best soups, nay, dishes, we have *ever* had. PERIOD! The bar is a pleasant old time saloon with a good selection. Great way to end a long and fun filled, awe inspiring day.

In the morning, we went up to the train yard. Chama is the headquarters of the Cumbres & Toltec Scenic RR. It uses restored Denver & Rio Grande narrow gauge steam engines and cars. Unfortunately for us, they only run in the summer, but at least we got the chance to poke around the yard without a lot of people in the way. This was a special part of the trip. My great grandfather was an engineer in the D&RG and was killed in a train wreck. Pretty cool to see a bit of family history. Well worth a trip on its own. We found a coffee place for muffins and headed north out of Chama towards Colorado. HUH?

The original idea was to take 64 south and east to Tres Pedras and Taos. Not in the winter ya don't. Road Closed Seasonally. So, Colorado bound we were. North on 17 following the tracks to Antonito, the other end of the railroad, then south on US 285, joining US 64 at tres Pedras. It's a worthwhile drive. Fabulous scenery and a good look at the Rockies.

We got to Taos and were under-impressed. Its pretty Yuppified (not as bad as Sedona, AZ) and we just didn't see anything worth stopping for. Maybe another day. From there, we followed the main road to Santa Fe. We did run across another of those serendipity moments at a roadside "museum" called "Classical Gas." Run by Johnnie Meier, its a collection of old gas station stuff. Everything from a variety of gas pumps to old oil cans and road maps, mostly for sale. Great guy. We had lunch in Santa Fe and poked around the old part of town. Also worth doing. Great galleries and jewelry stores and "Stuff."

From this point on, it was mostly the dreaded interstate. We had dreams of staying in Winslow, AZ, but after the traffic of Albuquerque (Helluva place to have to spell), we rolled into Gallup, NM after dark, and we rolled into a *Treasure*. The El Rancho Hotel. Stopping Place for Movie Stars! Headquarters for most of the movie crews that filmed in the area. It's a real slice of the high end dining and accommodations from the hey day of Route 66. *Do Not Miss This Place.* We stayed in the cheaper motel annex, but had dinner in the hotel. Best Enchiladas *ever*, except maybe my Mother-in-Law's. I'll tell ya though, it was a close call.

Next morning, we headed out of town and sure enough, got bit by the serendipity bug again. We were looking for coffee and doughnuts and BAM, there it was. A doughnut place, surrounded by local vehicles. Always a good sign. Great fresh sinkers and BONUS, FRESH MADE, STILL WARM FLOUR TORTILLAS!

Next on the agenda was the Petrified Forest. Just over the Arizona border, it's worth every penny of the $10 fee to drive through. Views of the Painted Desert, then south, crossing the freeway through the oddest rock formations *ever*. Petrified trees in colors you would think impossible outside of a Crayola box. In fact, they looked like some giant's kids had left their crayons out in the sun and melted all over the rocks. Great stuff. As we left the bottom of the park, we hit US Highway 180, north to Holbrook (which looks worth

Who can resist such a great place in Holbrook, AZ?
photo by the author

exploring on its own, a real funky Route 66 feel about the main drag) and saw the oddest highway sign I've ever seen. "Caution!--Road Not Patrolled!" I think they thought it was a warning. I naturally took it to mean permission. I mean, hell, if they're gonna let ya know ahead of time that they don't bother to keep tabs… I'll let you figure out the rest. Of course if you mess up, your bones will bleach in the summer sun. Your call.

We finally (well, it didn't take very long, really) got back on I-40 West and headed home. This is where the radar detector saved us a bunch of bucks and grief. Williams to the California border is *very* heavily patrolled. They are even adding in *speed cameras*. Those dirty %@$&#*s. Be warned.

All in all, we covered a *huge* amount of territory that is worth spending a whole lot more time in. Get out there (summer is probably too hot and too crowded) and discover what John Ford returned to again and again, trying to convey on film: the endless majesty of the Wild West.

Great Arizona/New Mexico Turquoise Trek-Directions Day One

HEAD NORTH on N Santa Anita Ave	0.8 mi
TURN RIGHT to merge onto I-210 E toward San Bernardino	11.8 mi
CONTINUE on CA-210 E	18.2 mi
EXIT I-15 N toward Barstow	67.5 mi
CONTINUE on I-40 E (signs for I-40/Needles)	

Entering Arizona — 199 mi

TAKE EXIT 44 for Shinarump Rd toward Oatman Hwy	0.4 mi
RIGHT on Historic U.S. 66 E	161 ft
LEFT to stay on Historic U.S. 66 E	5.0 mi
RIGHT on W Andy Devine Ave	11.5 mi
CONTINUE on AZ-66 E	78.6 mi
LEFT to merge onto I-40 E toward Flagstaff	38.2 mi
TAKE EXIT 161 for US-66 toward I-40 BUS/Willliams/Grand Canyon	0.4 mi
RIGHT on Historic U.S. 66 E	1.3 mi

This is Williams, AZ. Lots of Motels to choose from.

Turquoise Trek-Day Two Directions

HEAD NORTHWEST on W Bill Williams Ave/Grand Canyon Ave/E Railroad Ave toward N 4th St	1.2 mi
CONTINUE on Historic U.S. 66 E	1.3 mi
RIGHT to merge onto I-40 E	29.1 mi
TAKE EXIT 195 toward Arizona 89A N/Flagstaff	0.7 mi
MERGE onto I-17 N	0.3 mi
CONTINUE on S Milton Rd	1.5 mi
CONTINUE on I-40 BUS E/Old Santa Fe/E Santa Fe Ave	0.2 mi
HEAD EAST on I-40 BUS E/E Santa Fe Ave/US-89 N toward N Beaver St Continue to follow US-89 N	66.6 mi
RIGHT on Navajo Trail/US-160 E	82.0 mi
LEFT on US-163 N	1.4 mi
LEFT toward Comb Ridge Rd	0.1 mi
TAKE 1st LEFT on Comb Ridge Rd	59 ft
CONTINUE EAST on Comb Ridge Rd toward US-163 S	0.3 mi
TAKE 2nd LEFT onto US-163 N	

Entering Utah — 62.9 mi

RIGHT on Bluff Rd/US-191 S

Entering Arizona — 26.4 mi

LEFT on US-160 E	28.2 mi
CONTINUE on US-64 E	

Entering New Mexico — 26.1 mi

LEFT on US-491 N/US-64 E — 17.2 mi

Directions continued on next page

The Great Turquoise Trek Day Two Directions, Continued

RIGHT ON Co Rd 6698	0.1 mi
CONTINUE on Co Rd 6100	3.7 mi
CONTINUE on Rd 6100	0.5 mi
CONTINUE on Co Rd 6100	1.6 mi
RIGHT on Co Rd 6100/NM-489 E	2.5 mi
CONTINUE on W Main St	2.2 mi
RIGHT on W Murray Dr/US-64 Bypass E	3.2 mi
CONTINUE on W Broadway Ave/US-64 E	82.4 mi
RIGHT on Jicarilla Blvd/US-64 E (signs for US-64/Chama Espanola/Santa Fe)	13.1 mi
RIGHT on US-64 E/US-84 S	12.4 mi
LEFT on NM-17 N	1.4 mi
LEFT on 5th St	

This is Chama, NM

Turquoise Trek-Day Three Directions

CONTINUE on NM-17 N	
Entering Colorado	8.2 mi
CONTINUE on CO-17 N	38.9 mi
CONTINUE on US-285 N	28.9 mi
RIGHT on 6th St	0.7 mi
LEFT on Denver Ave/US-160 E	24.8 mi
RIGHT on CO-159 S/Miranda Ave	
Entering New Mexico	33.7 mi
CONTINUE on NM-522 S	41.1 mi
CONTINUE on Paseo Del Pueblo Norte/US-64 E	4.0 mi
LEFT on Barela Ln	180 ft
TAKE 1st RIGHT to stay on Barela Ln	253 ft
This is Taos, NM	
HEAD SOUTHWEST on Barela Ln toward Kit Carson Rd	82 ft
RIGHT on Kit Carson Rd	144 ft
LEFT on NM-68 S/Paseo Del Pueblo Sur	45.3 mi
SLIGHT RIGHT on S Riverside Dr	1.0 mi
CONTINUE on US-285 S/US-84 S	26.5 mi
TAKE RAMP onto I-25 S	56.2 mi
TAKE EXIT 226B to merge onto I-40 W toward Gallup	136 mi
TAKE EXIT 22 toward Miyamura Dr/Montoya Blvd	0.2 mi
KEEP LEFT at the fork, follow signs for Central Business District	190 ft
LEFT on Ford Dr	0.2 mi
CONTINUE on Miyamura Opas	174 ft
CONTINUE on S Ford Dr	312 ft
RIGHT on E Aztec Ave	

This is the El Rancho Hotel, Gallup, NM
Day Four Directions on next page.

Road Trippin'

The Great Turquoise Trek, Day Four Directions
To Leave Gallup, NM:

HEAD WEST on I-40 BUS W/NM-118 W toward S 2nd St	184 ft
TAKE 1st RIGHT onto S 2nd St	0.2 mi
TAKE 2nd LEFT on W Maloney Ave/NM-609	0.9 mi
TAKE 2nd LEFT on US-491 S	262 ft
MERGE onto I-40 W via the ramp to Flagstaff	
Entering Arizona	68.5 mi
TAKE EXIT 311 toward Petrified Forest/National Park	0.4 mi
RIGHT toward Petrified Forest Rd	6.0 mi
CONTINUE STRAIGHT onto Petrified Forest Rd	22.5 mi
RIGHT on US-180 W	17.5 mi
RIGHT on Apache Ave	0.7 mi
CONTINUE on Navajo Blvd.	1.0 mi
RIGHT to merge onto I-40 W toward Flagstaff	

From here, just go home, stopping for neat stuff along the way. There is plenty to see.

Monument Valley, Northern
Arizona
photo by the author

The Pacific Northwest

Wow, now this is a really different area. One that few people in SoCal would even *think* of. There are problems as well. The obvious one is how to get there in the first place. The second, how to get home. Those two minor details are addressed in the last couple of chapters on Highways 395 and 101. For now, let's focus on what is available in the PacNoWest.

Now despite the fact that there is only one north-south freeway between Olympia and Seattle, there are a bunch of great side roads featuring both mountains and seaside. If you pick the right time of year, you can spot whales and orcas off the coast or even in the Puget Sound itself. The only drawback (?) is that trees line the roads so much that you can't see if there is anything beyond them. At times, it's a kind of tunnel vision, a fir lined canyon. Certainly different from the wide open vistas of Monument Valley. Since I have family in Oly, I'm basing the directions from there. Most involve I-5 in someway or

Wiammette/Shay, Climax, and Mikado at the Mt. Rainier Scenic Railway photo by author

t'other so finding your way to the good drives won't be hard.

By the way, when in Olympia, check out the Speedway Brewing Company in nearby Lacey, WA. WOW, some of the best BBQ on the trip. The owner, Brett Dodd, made a living filming car races in Europe. His dad was a local drag racing legend. The place is filled with Racer Stuff and the food and beer are truly wonderful.

So, here's three Road Trip gems up in the soggy corner of the west coast.

Olympic Peninsula Tour

Let's start with a lap around the Olympic Peninsula. This is a gorgeous drive with lots to see and good food to boot. This will take you up one side of the Hood Canal. If the day is clear, this is a spectacular drive. There are any number of neat places to explore along the way. Pick a few likely spots and see what happens. You might want to break up this part of the journey, depending on how much coffee you had in the morning. There are long stretches without places to pee, so time things well.

Port Townsend is an old whaling port, but now is a great tourist destination. Lots of fun shops and good food to boot. I *highly* recommend the Belmont Hotel

Now THAT'S a bar stool! Speedway Brewing Co., Lacey WA
photo by the author

Restaurant. The Blue Cheese Lovers Salad and the Cioppino are out of this world. In fact, all the sea food is great. From there, its a short jaunt to Port Angeles, another whaling port, but also an old US Army fort, positioned to guard the top of the Puget Sound. If I recall, US Grant was stationed there at one time before the Civil War. This is also a charming tourist town now and worth a stop. Along the way are other neat towns, Sequim (pronounced "skwim" by to locals, so don't blow it!), Forks, and Humptulips (I'm *not kidding*!), then Aberdeen. From there its a straight shot back to Olympia. It would be easy to make this a two day jaunt. There are lots of places to stay along the way.

This upper corner of the country has a lot to offer the Road Tripper. Great roads, great people (they *do, however,* tend to drive *right* at the speed limit or less), great scenery and great food.

69

Olympic Peninsula Tour-Directions

TAKE the I-5 S towards Portland	0.7 mi
TAKE EXIT 104 to merge onto US-101 N	6.1 mi
SLIGHT RIGHT to stay on US-101 N	
(signs for US-101 N/Shelton/Port Angeles)	78.0 mi
RIGHT on WA-20 W (signs for Satte Route 20 E/Port Townsend)	7.8 mi
LEFT on Airport Cutoff Rd/WA-19 N/WA-20 E	
Continue to follow WA-20 E	4.8 mi
CONTINUE on Water St	0.2 mi

This is Port Townsend, WA

To Leave Port Townsend:

HEAD SOUTHWEST on Water St toward Tyler St	0.5 mi
CONTINUE on E Sims Way/WA-20 W	4.4 mi
RIGHT to stay on WA-20 W	7.8 mi
SLIGHT RIGHT on Olympic Hwy/US-101 W	32.5 mi
RIGHT on E Front St	1.6 mi
LEFT on N Lincoln St/US-101 W (signs for US-101 W/Forke)	1.0 mi
CONTINUE STRAIGHT on E Lauridsen Blvd/US-101 W	158 mi
SLIGHT RIGHT on Lincoln St	0.8 mi
Lincoln St turns SLIGHTLY and becomes 5th St	0.1 mi
LEFT on Simpson Ave/US-101 S	3.2 mi
LEFT on W Heron St	0.7 mi
LEFT on S G St	367 ft
FIRST LEFT on E Wishkah St	413 ft

This is Aberdeen, WA

HEAD SOUTHWEST on E Wishkah St toward S I St	312 ft
TAKE 1st LEFT onto S I St	367 ft
TAKE 1st LEFT E Heron St	0.4 mi
CONTINUE on Olympic Hwy/E Wishkah Blvd	
Continue to follow Olympic Hwy	20.8 mi
CONTINUE on W Simpson Svr/WA-8 E	20.7 mi
CONTINUE on US-101 S	5.5 mi
EXIT onto I-5 N toward Olympia/Seattle	

Centralia and the Coast

An easier day trip is south from Olympia to Centralia. This is may be my favorite town in Washington. I *love* the place. When my folks first moved up there, I was out chasing trains and came across this wonderfully charming town with a *great* train station. Twenty years ago, the town was a bit sad. The Sprawl-Mart on the interstate had killed most of the businesses that the virtual death of the lumber industry hadn't already ruined. There were a handful of pawn shops, seedy bars, and empty store fronts. The town has reinvented itself into a Destination. There's a *ton* of antique stores (several have not done well recently in the recession, but Marianne *did* find (surprise) turquoise and I found a RR Signal lamp) and the Olympic Club has become THE cool place to be. Seems there is a PacNW entrepreneur by the name of McMenimine, who buys old hotels and brings them back to their former glory. The Olympic has a rather checkered past but has now become a very good eatery, hotel and movie house, specializing in movies of the 30s and 40s.

Take I-5 SOUTH to Mellen St. (exit 81) and go left. Follow Mellen to Alder St. Go Left on Alder then right on Cherry. The main drag is Tower. Turn Left. There is plenty of public parking. Since it''s only a half hour from Olympia, head out after breakfast, cruise the stores, and have lunch. After lunch, if you're up to another jaunt. Head back to I-5, go south on I-5 to WA-6 (exit 77) to Raymond. There's a great little town with more antique shops (are you sensing a theme to the PacNW?) called PeEll. Named after some guy whose initials were P.L! *Really.* Raymond is an interesting place. Look for the weathered steel cut outs of people and cows and stuff. Kinda different. From Raymond there are two choices. You can head north on 101 to Aberdeen, then back to Olympia, or west on WA105 towards Westport, then back to Aberdeen. Either way, its a great little drive.

Road Trippin'

Centralia and the Coast-Directions

Head SOUTH on I-5 S towards Portland	22.4 mi
TAKE EXIT 82 for Harrison Ave	0.3 mi
KEEP LEFT at the fork, follow signs for City Center	144 ft
LEFT on Harrison Ave	0.8 mi
CONTINUE on W Main St	0.6 mi
LEFT on N Tower Ave	144 ft

This is Centralia, WA

HEAD NORTH on N Tower Ave toward W Pine St	217 ft
TAKE 1st LEFT on W Pine St	315 ft
TAKE 1st LEFT on N Pearl St	0.4 mi
RIGHT on W Cherry St	0.2 mi
LEFT at the 1st cross street onto Alder St	0.3 mi
RIGHT on Mellen St	0.4 mi
LEFT to merge onto I-5 S toward Portland	3.4 mi
TAKE EXIT 77 for WA-6 W toward Raymond/Pe E11	0.3 mi
RIGHT on Main St/WA-6 W	22.9 mi
RIGHT on W 4th Ave/WA-6 W	28.3 mi
RIGHT on US-101 N	0.9 mi
LEFT on Park Ave/WA-105 N	30.1 mi
RIGHT to stay on WA-105 N	18.2 mi
LEFT to stay on WA-105 N	0.1 mi
CONTINUE NORTH on US-101 N	0.6 mi
LEFT on E Wishkah St	413 ft

This is Aberdeen, WA

HEAD SOUTHWEST on E Wishkah St toward S I St	312 ft
TAKE 1st LEFT on S I St	367 ft
TAKE 1st LEFT on E Heron St	0.4 mi
CONTINUE on Olympic Hwy/E Wishkah Blvd	20.8 mi
CONTINUE on W Simpson Svr/WA-8 E	20.7 mi
CONTINUE on US-101 S	5.5 mi
EXIT onto I-5 N toward Olympia/Seattle	

Mt. Rainier Scenic Railway

A third great day out with a pleasant drive thrown in is to Elbe, WA (you guessed it, named for a guy whose initials were L.B.) and the Mount Rainier Scenic Railway. You just *knew* I'd throw more trains in somehow. This place is *great*. Real steam locomotives, and not your everyday, run of the mill locos, logging locos. They have an operating Climax *and* perhaps the only operating Willamette in the world. These are *crazy* to watch. I got lucky and made it up there on a day they hooked the Climax, the Willamette, and a 2-8-2 tank locomotive all together to pull a tourist special. The Mikado was a standard side rod loco like most of you are used to. The Climax has an angled piston/rod assembly geared to a crankshaft, then to drive shafts to the wheels. The Willamette has 3 vertical cylinders connected to an external crank, thence to gears that drive the wheels. I'm telling you, I haven't seen that much motion since I once (*Long* before marriage) saw twin strippers counter-rotate the tassel twirling! *Amazing*! Eat in Mineral at the old school house. A couple of gals have turned the old cafeteria in to a cafe. Good Burger, Good Ribs, *Great* People.

Mt. Rainier Scenic Railway Tour

NORTH on I-5 N toward Seattle	6.0 mi
TAKE EXIT 111 for Marvin Rd S toward Yelm	0.5 mi
At the traffic circle, take the 2nd exit onto Quinault Dr NE	0.2 mi
RIGHT on Marvin Rd NE/WA-510 E	1.5 mi
At the traffic circle, take the 2nd exit onto Pacific Ave SE/WA-510 E	
Continue to follow WA-510 E	11.4 mi
CONTINUE on WA-507 N/E Yelm Ave	
Continue to follow WA-507 N	2.9 mi
RIGHT on 352nd St S/Mc Kenna Tanwax/WA-702 E	9.3 mi
RIGHT on Mountain Hwy E/National Park Hwy/WA-7 S	19.1 mi
HEAD SOUTHEAST on Mountain Hwy E/National Park Hwy/WA-7 S toward 542 St E/542nd St E	0.2 mi
TAKE 1st RIGHT on WA-7 S	0.5 mi
TAKE 1st LEFT on Mineral Hill Rd	3.2 mi
CONTINUE on Mineral Rd N	0.1 mi

4.0 mi – about 10 mins

This is Mineral, WA

HEAD SOUTH on Mineral Rd S toward Maple Ln	1.6 mi
LEFT on WA-7 S	11.2 mi
HEAD SOUTH on 2nd St/WA-7 S toward Main Ave	0.5 mi
RIGHT on US-12 W (signs for US-12 W/Mossyrock)	31.0 mi
RIGHT TO MERGE onto I-5 N/US-12 W toward Seattle	

Miscellaneous Light Reading
by the Fireside or Bedside or Looside

The following are from some of my columns in *The Automotive Calendar of Events*. I've been told they make for some good reading, but what do they know? Anyway, maybe they will inspire you to hit the road, help make your Road Trips better, or just plain amuse you.

"Route 66"-The TV Show

I thought I'd make a bit of a departure at this point, and do more of a review than a road trip. I found myself a Christmas present at Autobooks a couple of years ago. Its an obvious choice for something for me to review: Volume One, Season One of the ultimate Road Trip Show--Yes folks, the TV series "ROUTE 66." I saw it and of course *had* to have it. Since it's the ultimate Road Trip Show, maybe it will give you the feeling of how it was "back then."

This is one of those shows that a lot of people refer to, but I'm betting probably never saw. At best, it's been so long that the reality of the show has faded. To the best of my knowledge, it's never been picked up as a retro-rerun. TV Land, Nick-at Night, *et. al.* are too busy showing garbage from the 1970s and 80s (but what can we expect when K-EARTH is now playing--shudder--*disco* as "oldies!") to pay attention to the really great TV that was available in the 50s and 60s. "Route 66" is one of those forgotten gems.

The premise, to remind everyone, is that Tod Stiles (played by a *very* freckle faced Martin Milner, later of "Adam-12" fame) is the educated, privileged guy who had to leave Yale after his father died, leaving him penniless. The only thing he has left is his 1961 Corvette (actually, in the first episode, possibly the pilot, the car is a '60) and a need to roam. His odd-couple buddy is Buz Murdock (George Maharis), a tough guy from Hell's Kitchen who was raised in an orphanage. Together they roam the country, working odd jobs, getting their kicks, and along the way, changing people's lives. The show also show cased a number of future stars such as Suzanne Pleshette, Leslie Nielsen, Lee Marvin, Harvey Korman, Jack Lord, DeForest Kelly (!!) and Joey Heatherton, several getting the "Introducing" tag in the credits. There were some well known people as well, such as E.G. Marshall and Jack Warden. The cast lists were really impressive.

Now to be honest, I was a whole ten years old when the first season aired--1960 (OK, go ahead *do* the math), and don't really remember much of the show. I doubt that my folks watched the show that much, and back then, only the insanely rich had more than one TV. It was probably shown later than my bed time anyway. I do remember seeing a few episodes later on, but I can't say I really have much more than a vague memory of it. Seeing the first few episodes were a revelation. Its hard to remember when TV drama was so, well, *Dramatic*. This feeling is enhanced by the fact that each episode has a Title, shown in the opening credits. Titles like "The Lance of Straw," or "Man on the Monkey Board" seem a bit over the top today, but they give us the feel that each show is its own play. The three central characters are the same (Tod, Buzz, and the Road), and (unusual for the day) there is a continuity from one week to the next, following up on previous adventures. Each show, however, stands alone in its own right. Shot in glorious, high contrast black and white, the show had tons of close-ups on faces that showed Character, and acting that was done by

Wonder if Tod and Buzz stayed here?
photo by the author

performers who started on the live stage, rather than in commercials. The feel is more like "Twilight Zone " or "Combat. " This is not a s h o w spotlighting the light hearted hi-jinx of two dudes having a great old time, which is what we'd see today. Each episode is alive with situations that require our two heros to show far more maturity than would be expected in today's Life-Lite society. Sure, they're attracted to some pretty girls, but not in the openly sexual way of today's shows. They really are young gentlemen. Of course, the TV codes of the day insured that kind of respectful yearning.

There is also the theme and musical score by Nelson Riddle. The title track is of course famous (it is *not* however the song "Get Your Kicks on Route 66"), and its meant to have the feel of wheels (knock-off wire wheels, in this case--gotta be one of the few 'Vettes with that option!) spinning down the road, the feel of *wanderlust*. Which is of course the whole premise of the show.

The real stars to me are the settings. This show was shot almost entirely on location. It's a postcard from the past that shows an America of small towns and big dreams. It's a less crowded America that still has a pre-Vietnam War enthusiasm. Although most of the road shots seem like they are done on minor back roads, in reality, this is pre-interstate America. Main roads could be just two lanes of blacktop. Although the shots are generally composed so the real names of the towns are obscured, some locations aren't too hard to figure out. Bourbon Street in New Orleans, shrimp boats in the gulf, Grant's Pass in Oregon. All these places figure in the plot and form the backdrop for the drama. It's as if the show's creator, Sydney Silliphant scouted the location and wrote the story to fit.

Now about this time, you may have noticed that Louisiana and Oregon aren't on Route 66. Yeah. In fact, about the only time they are actually *on* Route 66 is in the third episode. The "Mother Road" was more of a metaphor for the wide expanse of the country. Each region of the US was still distinct in 1960, the commercial homogenization of America was only in its infancy, and the Highway connected far flung places that were rarely visited. It reminds me of the trips from LA to Sacramento up old Highway 99 to see my grandparents. There was distance between towns. Each town was distinct. The highway was the main street back then so we'd look for landmarks along the way that told us how far we'd come. "Water, Wealth. Contentment, Health" proclaimed the arching sign entering Modesto. The smell of olives in Lindsay, the Big Orange stands, Burma Shave signs with the punch line missing. My dad convinced that truck drivers knew the "good" places to eat. My sister, brother and I wedged firmly into our spots (well, nests) with favorite toys in reach to keep us busy. Who needed seat belts or airbags? They had to physically extract us and then rebury us at each potty stop. The hours long road games, like the geography game. (name a town, country, physical place anywhere in the world, no street names. The next person has to start theirs with the last letter of the last place, no repeats. Think that's easy? Wait till some

Restored to its former glory, the Cool Springs gas station near Oatman, AZ
photo by Marianne McCarthy

joker says, "Essex"). These treks ended when we crept past an accident in the tule fog. Christmas presents were scattered around an overturned 1955 Buick.

The show has this feeling of searching, of striving, of needing answers to life that perhaps are not really there. This is years before hippies and "do your own thing." These are two guys who were too young for WWII or Korea, but will be too old for Vietnam. They are button-down collar and dress slacks, not James Dean jeans and t-shirt guys. They are rebels of the heart, not of fashion. They are not Brando ("What are you rebelling against?"--"I don't know, what have you got?") guys, they are searchers. They are knights errant on a powder blue steed, tilting at life's windmills, but keeping to a code of honor that is their own.

Get yourself a copy and go back in time. You'll be ready to seek out those back roads and long shuttered main streets and try to peel back the layers of plastic and fast food that hide the America of our youth. After all, a bit of maudlin, nostalgic yearning is good for you,

Road Trip Music

"Son, you're gonna drive me to drinkin' if you don't stop drivin' that
Hot................Rod.................Lincoln!"

Clearly, the greatest Road Trip song of all time. But even as great as Charlie Ryan's (who sadly passed away recently at the age of 92) anthem to the Hot Rod is, you can't listen to it more than five of six times on a Road Trip without the danger of rebellion from the shotgun seat. So what other songs are essential on a road trip? Is, in fact, music even a necessary component to a Road Trip? If you drive a TR3 with Brooklands windscreens that make it impossible to hear (like we do), I'm guessing no. If your idea of a road trip involves anything that is red, Italian, and has 12 cylinders, you've got all the music you need from the tailpipes. If the V8 rumble and blower whine make you shout to be heard, probably not. But still, in most instances, music and Road Trips generally go together like Guinness and mussels in cream sauce.

Now it used to be, before the advent of satellite radio, that half the fun of a road trip was finding a radio station. Any radio station! In the bad ol' days of AM only radio, when there were three whole stations that were deemed acceptable to teens in LA (quick, for 50 points and a free trip to Pacoima, NAME THOSE STATIONS) if you were off in the boonies, you might be able to catch a skip off the ionosphere (or what ever sphere it is, science isn't my strong suit) and pick up Wolfman Jack, broadcasting from his secret lair somewhere around (so it was rumored) Waco, Texas. If you were unlucky, you got Grand Ol' Opry. I got the opportunity to demonstrate this lost art to my daughter, Brianna, as we were driving her newly acquired '62 Mercury Comet home from Hemet. We were cresting the Beaumont Pass and trying the radio. It only took 5 minutes for the tubes (Yes, *tubes*!) to warm up, then with that old familiar: "WEEEEEOOOOOOOOOWWWEEEEEUUUUUUUOOOOO" we managed to pick up something. A traffic report. For Salt Lake City! Needless to say, my daughter was impressed! Now we have multiple disc CD players, or iPods that can carry all the music of the Western World. What do you load in for that multi-day, cross country trek?

Obviously, personal tastes play the most important role, but still, music that is maybe a bit out of your comfort zone can enhance a road trip in ways unimaginable. Time of day is also a factor. So is weather. So is the road. So is the car. The only types not allowed in my cars are Disco and Hip Hop/Rap. I'm boycotting K-EARTH now that they've started to play the BeeGees as "Oldies." Puh! Overall though, the more eclectic your play list, the better the experience. So here's some of our favorites. It's far from a complete list. That would take enough space to fill several books..

For just plain cruisin', even if it's a day long drive, proper Rock and Roll is just the ticket. After all, that's how we all got started. Whether it was up and down Colorado in Pasadena or Whittier Blvd., or where ever, we all cruised to Rock and roll. Windows down, arm hanging out, Just Cruisin'. Some of the best collections can be had from a local DJ everyone around here knows as LeRoy, the Milkman. You've probably seen and heard him at various car shows around SoCal. He puts together some amazing CDs. My favorite is called LeRoy's Car Tunes. It's got almost every great car song ever, including of course, "Hot Rod Lincoln." There's "Little Deuce Coupe." "409," "Mustang Sally," and "Fun, Fun, Fun." Pretty much what *has* to be there is there (I can't figure out why "Dead Man's Curve: is missing, though), but he's included other, more obscure stuff as well: "Pink Cadillac," "Rocket 88," and "Bucket T," for starters. My next favorite of his is "Surf Tunes." A whole CD of the greatest surfer music ever. "Miserlou," "Wipe Out," "Telstar Surf!" It doesn't get much better than that! He also has several Doo-Wop CDs available, nice for the late night cruise, when you want to dial things back a bit on a warm summer night.

My next Rock and Roll selection is a truly varied compilation. I bought it at the Rose Bowl Swap meet, but I've seen the guy at other events. Its a four CD set put out by Invicta Music, Ltd., up in Quebec, Canada (of all places!). Who, knows, these may not yet be "Oldies" up there in the Great White North. Anyway, this set has 103 songs. It's at least three hours of music. Volume One begins with Willie Nelson and "On the Road Again," proceeds through Freddy Fender ("Before the Next Tear Drop Falls"), Creedence (Bad Moon Rising"), and The Diamonds ("Little Darlin'"), before hitting Duane Eddy, Jan and Dean, and Three Dog Night. It just gets better with Volume Two. Janis Joplin and "Bobby McGee" gives way to "Sixteen Tons" and Tennessee Ernie Ford. Bo Diddley, WAR, Chuck Berry and the Eagles also show up. Three and Four are equally as mixed up. Meatloaf, The Troggs, The Boss, Foghat, and the Vogues mix it up with Howlin' Wolf, the Doobie Brothers, and ZZ Top. Whew, makes me tired just listing the stuff. I have to tell you too, all the cuts on these CDs aren't in my comfort zone. Neil Diamond and Glen Campbell usually get bypassed, but that's just me.

"Sleep in a TeePee! The Wigwam Motel. A classic bit of Route 66 funk!
photo by the author

Now so far, we've stayed in an area that I'm betting is safe for most of you. Good Ol' Rock and Roll. Let's push the boundaries. Late at night, on a long lonely road, maybe with enough rain to need the wipers on real slow, try Jazz. Smooth, Cool, Jazz. Dave Brubeck, Wes Montgomery, Antonio Carlos Jobin. Spice it up a bit if you are really adventurous with some John Coltrain, or Miles Davis. There is something about 2 AM, an Open Road, and Jazz.

OK, now let's *really* push the limits. Let's go all out beyond what most people can deal with. It may surprise you. Opera. Yes, Opera. That-Thing-Foreigners-Do-Until-Your-Head-Hurts. In the words of Luciano Paverotti, "Controlled Screaming." I'm telling you, there is nothing like flying down a back road with that same Paverotti belting "Vin-c-her-a, Vin-c-her-AA, vin-CHHEERR--ah!" at the end of "Nesun Dorma" or carving up Highway One in the fog with Maria Callas doing the Mad Scene from "Lucia di Lammermoor." Its bloody *magic*! Vocal Classical a bit too much for you? Fine, try some instrumental stuff. Mozart symphonies are great stuff. Not too heavy, actually hum-able, yet very satisfying. I'd suggest Ravel's "Bolero," but that's not driving music, that's parking music.

Mr. D's in Kingman, AZ
a classic bit of nostalgia
photo by the author

The last genre I advise you to look into for variety is traditional Irish Music. Not "When Irish Eyes are Smiling," or "Danny Boy," but the *real* stuff. Try the Chieftains, especially their early albums. Its easy to tell which ones they are, they're numbered. As in "Chieftains 1." "Chieftains 2." and so on. Numbers 4, 5 and 8 are my personal favorites. Other groups like Dervish, Bothy Band, or Planxty are good bets. I'm telling ya, a good fast, hard reel has just the right rhythm for slamming up a mountain road.

Since a good sound system seems necessary for a good ride, find some good music to play on it. That's the beauty of modern technology, you can burn your own mixes at the 'puter. Van Morrison, Simon and Garfunkle, the Doors, some Motown. Throw in Cat Stevens and the Beatles and the Stones with Mozart and Puccini, a touch of Cannonball Adderly, a soupcon of Charlie Parker and you've got the right idea. Mix it up, and keep people guessing as they try to figure you out. And like they say, if its too loud, *you're* too old.

Ode to the Cannonball Baker, Sea-to-Shining-Sea Memorial Trophy Dash

Remember the Seventies? Neither do I. I spent *waaay* too much time and money in a local pub called The Loch Ness Monster killing brain cells with Guinness (when I could afford it-Pabst Blue Ribbon when I couldn't, which was most of the time). Heck, I didn't own a TV in the Seventies. A good thing too, ever see any of those horrible shows? What I *did* do in my non-drinking hours was drive a bus to get through college, drive the TR3 as my only car, and wish I had the dough to drive race cars. Naturally, I also read a magazine called Car and Driver. Now, youngsters, C/D was NOT the namby-pamby mag that it is today. Yeah, it's still smart ass but they road test SUVs fer cryin' out loud! Back then, this mag had *guts*! They bragged that a Pontiac GTO could out run a Ferrari GTO. They castigated the Opel Kadett as the blandest, lamest POS on the planet. Brock Yates, Leon Mandel, David E. Davis, Jr., and (God help me) *Jean Shepard* graced those pages with prose, piss, and vinegar that are unmatched by today's lobotomized bean-counter induced pabulum. Try and get a copy of Yates' masterpiece article on the meltdown of Detroit called "Grosse Pointe Myopians." It makes my friend and fellow columnist Merkle Weiss seem like a flag waver for US Iron. The Seventies (not the Sixties really) were a time of great social protest. Everybody seemed hell bent on hating *something* and *everything*. It was the fulfillment of Brando in "The Wild One"--"What are you rebelling against?" "I don't know, what a ya got?" Car and Driver led the ranks of automotive civil disobediancers and Brock Yates was the ring leader: "Gear Heads Unite, 55 MPH SUCKS!"

To lead this charge, Yates created the ultimate Road Trip. A kick in the teeth of Ralphie Nadar and Jill Clayburgh (remember *her?* Miss 55-MPH-Governors-on-All-Cars?) He called it after Erwin G. "Cannon Ball" Baker, renowned setter of cross country records in the teens and 20s when a cross country trip meant mostly unpaved roads. "The Cannonball Baker, Sea-to-Shining-Sea-Memorial-Trophy-Dash." A *race* (not a rallye, not a cruise, a RACE) from the Red Ball Garage on the lower east side of Manhattan to the Portofino Inn in Redondo Beach, CA. No prizes, just Glory. The idea was to prove that cross country travel in cars that were built for speed and driven by capable drivers could be done at high speed and no carnage would occur. Ahh, those were the days.

All this came back to me whilst perusing the shelves at everybody's favorite automotive book store, Autobooks. The book jumped into my hands. "Cannonball!-World's Greatest Outlaw Road Race," by the mastermind hisself--Brock Yates (copyright 2002, Motorbooks International, isbn #0-7603-1633-3--get Tina to order one for you if they are out of stock). OOOOOOBABY--Come to PAPA! This is the real, true, unvarnished story. Its not those utterly stooopid movies (one actually written and OK'd by Yates), it's not the BS spouted by your buddy about how *he* was in the Cannonball (by the way, there is a BS indicator in the appendix--the names, dates, finishing time, and vehicle of *every* true competitor. If your buddy's name ain't on the list, he's BSing you) This book is great! This book is hilarious! This book remembers when we were too young and too stupid to know better, had a great time, and lived to tell the tale.

The Author, Ready to Roll!
photo by Mike Andrews

Yates does most of the telling, but what is most fun are the tales of other competitors. There are pieces by Brad Niemcek (leader of the Polish Racing Drivers Association--they always started first, naturally claiming as a birthright the "Pole" position), Donna Mae Mims (if you remember her, *shame* on you for what you're thinking!), western stock car racer Jack McCoy, oh, and some guy named Dan Gurney. Believe me, Gurney's tale of hitting black ice at a buck and a quarter on a bridge in Arizona driving a Daytona Ferrari ("Glare ice! This is BLEEDING GLARE ICE!") is worth the price of the book alone. The fascinating thing here is comparing Yates' account with Gurney's. There are other tales of daring do and a few of daring don't: Yates wife strapped to a stretcher in an ambulance and getting the New Jersey State Cops to buy their story--complete with the story from the cops themselves, Mims, Judy Stropus, and Peggy Niemecek rolling a limo, the guys who got a "drive-a-way" Caddie that needed delivery to the west coast, its all there.

What really hit home with me is how far we have come. The *de facto* speed limit is 80-85. A new Toyota Camry probably handles better than the Daytona Ferrari that Yates and Gurney drove cross country in just under 36 hours. It won't do 174 mph, but at 80, most new cars are comfortable and easy to drive and are far more reliable than most of what we drove in the 70s. The Interstate system is pretty much complete, and nobody drives through the main drag of East Overshoe, OK anymore. The irony is that Brock Yates himself, in the Afterword, feels that an endeavor like the Cannonball could not be duplicated today. The traffic density of cities is too great for one thing. LA is a good example. Remember when Cucamunga and Chino were in the boonies? Hell, people are commuting from *Beaumont* and see *no* open land into LA! Except for Camp Pendleton, there isn't any open space to speak of all the way to San Diego. This alone would doom a record setting run (beat 32 hours?) and 30 hours is out of the question.

Or is it? Use Google Maps and check the various routes. Radar/laser detectors have gotten pretty sophisticated. The Interstate system was supposedly designed for speeds far higher than are allowed. The Cannonball was also run in *November*! ARE YOU MAD? Weather played a role in many a delay. Of course, adding gas tanks to extend range is a bit trickier than adding several 10 gallon jerry cans to the trunk, as one poor soul did, so some refined re-engineering beyond duct tape and fuel hoses would be needed. Tire construction is also vastly superior. Given some good luck and a *lot* of preplanning using baskets of local traffic knowledge (and we have the internet today, don't we?) one just might be able to break 32 hours. Hmmmmmmm.

At least get the book and journey back to the time. Revel in the insanity of the "World's Greatest Outlaw Road Race."

Some people are just CRAZY! Paul Anderson gets ready to slog some
backroads
photo by Marianne McCarthy

Best Roads Ever Survey

Wouldja like to take a survey? I posed this to a random set of people about the roads they liked. I figured that I've nattered along about so many of my favorites, that its high time to give others a chance to sound off on the topic. Unsurprisingly, the suggestions were widely varied. Surprisingly, well maybe not *that* big a surprise, were a couple of constants. The top vote getter, in *every* category was Hwy 101. Almost every respondent mentioned one section or another of what may well be the best damn road in America. A few years ago, we packed the whole family up for a "Last Major Family Road Trip" to Olympia, WA for my dad's 80th birthday. We did 101 *all the way up*. Took three days with stops in Salinas and Crescent City. Did I mention that we used 2 cars? The Trusty Blue Meanie and my wife's Mitsubishi Lancer as a chase/support car. Everyone took turns riding shotgun in the TR3. I naturally did all the driving in it. I'm here to tell ya, that was one *Hell* of a trip! So, yeah, not much beats 101. Its got it all.

So, enough of what I like, what did you all like? Some people added comments, so I'll leave them in, pretty much unedited and in no particular order.

Favorite Tight and Twisty Roads:

1. Route 130--(Alum Rock Road) from San Jose to route 5
2. The section of 101 just north of Ft Bragg
3. Banner Road Southwest Riverside County. Banner is nothing more than a post office but the road to it has one really good heel/toe-right/left section that's just bitchin' - but only going down hill. I liked it so much I drove back up and did it again. Getting there is not really worth the effort however. Lots of curves, steep grades and scenery.
4. Glenwood Canyon in Colorado. Long sweeping curves and decent speed.
5. CA Hwy 299 between Redding and Eureka, CA
6. CA Hwy 49 between Mariposa and Placerville – I did that one in '76 on my 1944 Chief.
7. The longest stretch of straight road [90 miles without a hint of a curve] is on the Nullabor Plains ... which means its the most boring godforsaken place on earth! But hey! you should try driving on the other really straight roads! Oh did I mention that there is a slight dogleg bend in our street! (there's always a wise guy! Ah, them Aussies!)
8. SR-1 from Morro Bay to Monterey (DUH!)
9. I don't consider tight and twisted roads as good ... they are dangerous and are an impediment to safe trips, so the word "best" is a misnomer. However, there are few short places where you can grapple with the steering wheel and floor pedals ...Up in Queensland, and west of Mackay is the beautiful Eungella National Park ... to get to it you have to drive up a narrow [in places only 1 car wide] "road" that crosses through floodways [or waterfalls] ... the climb starts at 200m above sea-level and goes up to 700m in about a mile as the crow flies, but is somewhat longer as you zig zag your way up the sheer precipice. The road has been

washed away several times by torrential rain, and each time it costs the earth to repair it (Again from a friend in OZ!).

10. CA 22 Moorpark to Fillmore

11. Angeles Crest (Again, DUH!)

Favorite high speed drives:

1. Again Hwy 299, but from Alturas to Shasta
2. US 97 from Klamath Falls to Weed
3. The road up to Mt Palomar
4. 146 mph on Highway 14 about 4 miles south of Mojave (not ME!)
5. I-90 across Montana - the average speed is the same as the highway number
6. Anywhere I had an empty Crown Coach and a couple of good friends. I'll give you the serious one later but it's probably Hwy 50 anywhere east of Bishop.
7. US 395 from Mojave to Reno
8. Smith Valley Rd, north of Bridgeport, CA
9. Nurburgring (!!!)
10. Lockwood Valley Rd.

ED Pasini, co-disorganizer on the Iron Bottom
and his 356
photo by the author

Scenery. Here is where 101 REALLY shines

1. US 101 through the tunnel at Gaviota--and north in spring
2. I-70 Utah / Colorado
3. Fraser Canyon in British Columbia between Hope and Kamloops - white water, tunnels, trains.
4. Both sides of the Hudson River in New York between Croton-Harmon and Albany, NY - trains, mountains, a *big* river with vessels, lots of great eats along the way, old churches, man do I miss the fall back there.
5. Sand Hills of Nebraska, Highway 2 I think, Ravenna, NE - trains and trees, hills and lakes.
6. Hwy 101 between Cloverdale and Eureka including Avenue of the Giants (do this in an open car or motorcycle. OMG!)
7. Probably the Ocean Road in Victoria that connects Melbourne to Adelaide. Distracted drivers and their cars are collected by local fishing trawlers as part of the annual "Clean Up Australia Day."
8. This is a hard one, because there are just so many to pick from, but Eungella National Park, Queensland is beautiful.
9. Chuckanut Drive, south of Fairfield/Bellingham, WA. Right along the water most of the way, beautiful views of the Islands of Puget Sound, BN Railway line, former Interurban line now a hiking trail, a "there's no alternative" route even though I-5 would be much, much faster.In good weather is gorgeous, in a gale the trees will occasionally throw branches and leaves at you but even then it's spectacular.
10. CA 33 to Ojai
11. South entrance of Sequoia National Park

Road Trippin'

What's a road trip without funky places to stop? Roadside attractions:

1. Trees of Mystery, Hwy 101, almost at the Oregon border. A CLASSIC!
2. Legend of Big Foot, also on 101, north of Willits
3. Carhenge outside Alliance, Nebraska
4. Integratron -Big Rock (by 29 palms)
5. Hwy 101 vicinity of Piercy, CA
6. In Australia, we have a lot of the things you see along American freeways and byways. One of the typical Aussie features is our penchant for having the biggest of anything by which a town can earn its place on the map and attract the tourist. For example the Big Pineapple is one such place, but there is the Big Sheep, the Big Prawn [Shrimp], the Big Banana, etc. However, the vineyards of Australia produce some of the best wine in the world and they cater for the tourist and winelover with free wine tasting.
7. CA 49 from Oakhurst to Grass Valley

The BEST roads have NO lines!
photo by Marianne McCarthy

8. Vineyard Road, off Highway 101 (again!) Try the Bella Luna Winery.
9. The whole town of Cayucos, CA, just north of Morro Bay.

The last category is the most essential. FOOD! What's a good road trip without good food?

1. Taco Temple in Morro Bay
2. Cosimo's on Union - Newburgh and Poughkeepsie, NY - truly great pizza and Italian
3. The Piggy Bank Newburgh, NY (next to Hew Haven branch station in an old bank building, wine cellar is in the vault, BBQ is most excellent.
4. There's another BBQ joint in Milan, NY but the name escapes me (it's been way too long, I need to go back).

5. Samoa Cookhouse - Eureka, CA - homestyle, best vegetable beef soup on Planet Urth !

6. On the Nullabor you just stop anywhere and help yourself to the free roadside cuisine ... for 88 kms [=50 + miles] you have a choice of feral camel, wombat and kangaroos. Mind you, you may have to watch out for speeding traffic as you flip it over to cook the other side and shoo away the flies and a few crows and eagles, but it beats having to catch them. (Ah, them crazy Aussies are at it again. Must be from being upside down all their lives)

7. I doubt if any roadside establishment in Australia will qualify as a great food outlet. The American fast food chains have just about killed the Aussie hamburger, fish and chips [french fries] cafe. Unlike a lot of US motels, Australian motels offer cooked breakfasts at a price. Best place to try are the local pubs in the small towns. We stayed overnight in Peterborough, SA which is an old railway town that is slowly dying. For just $13 each we bought a generous roast lamb dinner with roast veggies that covered a large size dinner plate, crepe desserts and a cup of tea [or coffee]. I was full and had no room for anything else other than probably a port and a bit of cheese. However, you have to search out such eateries.

8. Pacific Coast Highway (PCH) there are loads of great dining places all along this classic route.

9. Worker Bee Cafe in Carpinteria for breakfast, for lunch, The Spot.

10. Jocko's in Nipomo!!!!! Just off good old 101. Best steak *on the planet*!

So, the results are in and tallied, the judges' decisions are final. Go out and find these gems and more.

The roads in Arizona may be a bit straight, but the scenery is
spectacular!
photo by Marianne McCarthy

Worst Roads Survey

Yep, *worst* drives. First, some ground rules--they can't be normal freeway commutes, that's just too easy, and fist fights would break out between haters of the 405 and the 91. Figures, two hot beds of road rage if there ever were any! No, let's look at the long grinds. The drives we really hate to make.

First and foremost has to be I-5 to NoCal. If *ever* there was a more benighted, moron infested, dull as dishwater drive, I haven't driven it. Even from its "grand" opening, its' been a horror. Three hundred miles of scenery only a Nebraskan can love, nothing to eat but the usual suspects of corporate glop with the glories of the Grapevine at one end and those cow pens at the other. Two lanes each way mean that the trucker who has to go 56 mph and is passing the "slow" one who is at 54 takes about three days to get around and backs up traffic for days. The yabbo who is determined that if 70 mph is indeed the speed limit, he has a perfect right to go 68 in the "fast" lane to teach those durn Speed Merchants of Death a lesson is another favorite. Add in the *other* yabbo how needs to go 95 and pass everything on the right and *boy* it makes for a "fun" drive. Put the whip cream on in the form of Chippies out to single handedly balance the state budget with speeding tickets and the cherry on top of Tule Fog in the winter and...Well, you get the picture.

Tough to top that one, but a close second is I-15 to Vegas. Add turn around gamblers' buses driven by guys who got a license out of a Crackerjacks box to the dim-bulbs who are determined to "make time" to Lost Wages so they can throw their money at happily receptive billionaire casino owners and the usual parade of truckers, most of whom can drive just fine, but enough of whom can't and you get a wonderfully nasty trip. The Interstate also bypassed anything of possible interest (most people think that the train station in Barstow is that cheesy Mickey D's at the junction of the 15 and the 40, rather than the spectacular El Desierto that the city fathers wish they could turn into a fine dining experience, but I digress) and corporate slop houses (when they have to add "beef flavoring" to their hamburgers and sugar to their carefully excreted fries, ya gotta wonder why?), allegedly cheap outlet stores, and gas stations are about it.

Third place goes to the I-10 from Phoenix to the California border. Characterless as the rest, the traffic anywhere near Px-Town is nasty and naturally, the whole thing is lined with the dull sameness of the other two. Gosh, do you sense a theme here? How have we allowed ourselves to be deluded into thinking that McJackKing serves anything edible, let alone deserve the name "Restaurant?" Madison Avenue's credo, borrowed from a certain doctor named Goebbles--"If you tell a lie often enough, people will believe it" seems to have plenty of validity.

The other's are tamer, but still bad: The Santa Barbara Crawl--south on the 101 through Santa Barbara and sometimes slow all the way to La Conchita. One wonders if taking out the stop light at State Street was worth it. Or how about the I-5 between Olympia, WA and Seattle? Yeah, I know, for most it's a commute but man, there is only one traffic corridor between Oly and Seattle. Add SeaTac Airport and over caffeinated Pacific Northwest Yuppies and it just takes one dope in his precious Beemer to snarl the thing for days, and there is no way around! Oh, and don't forget, some moron speced an experimental concrete that is now so worn by truck tires that there is a truck wide twin trough up the whole way. If you have a narrow car, say a certain TR3, one wheel is in a trough, the other on a crown. We felt like we were tilted about 30 degrees off level!

Then there is the Bay Area. All of it. Did the same CalTrans that actually did a good job setting up the directional signs down here have anything to do with the Bay Area? Is it some kind of hyper-liberal-eco-nazi's plot to force us out of our evil polluting death traps? Do they make the traffic worse up there on purpose? Does the famous Frisco Fog stay in driver's heads replacing brains? Does eating vegan granola impede the ability to drive?

From the top of Naciemento-Fergueson Road. Who spilled the pasta down the hillside?
photo by Marianne McCarthy

Speaking of granola eating ex-hippies, there is the entire state of Oregon. You know 'em--they drive around here with the license plate with the big tree on it that looks like they're flipping you off. Them's the ones, either doing 45 in the fast lane of the 210 or 95 weaving in and out of traffic like a slalom racer. Worst drivers *ever!* Ya know, they won't let you pump your own gas up there. They have to employ some chowder head to do it for you so he can slop gas down the fender of your multi K paint job. There is a possible amusement factor here, however. I'm betting that driving a '53 Caddy with the gas filler in the tail light must be worth hours of entertainment value. They don't have Highway Patrol up there either. Its the "State Police"! *How verry DDR off zem.* My favorite part is the obvious fact that someone in the highway department must have a worthless brother-in-law who owns a sign making company. The plethora of "Do Not Pass," "Seat Belt Laws Enforced," etc., etc, etc, is amazing! Are Oregonians that stupid that they need 4+ signs on each side of the road to let you know that the passing lane is ending? In addition that is to the lines and arrows on the road? Oh, and they still have suicide lanes up there! Are you old enough to remember a center lane for passing in both directions? They got their name (and banned here) for very good reason. Top that off with trucks with triple trailers and the whole state, despite some really great scenery could disappear and we'd all be better off.

Whew, what led to the snark-fest? Maybe its because as I wrote this originally, school was starting and I had to get it out of my system. Maybe I watch too much Anthony Bourdain. Maybe I need more (or less) bran in my diet. At any rate, I hope you got at least a giggle out of all this. If not, don't call me, call 1-(800) Tough Luck.

The Great Route 66 Field Trip

Tina at Autobooks was appalled. "You're doing WHAT?" She shuddered visibly.

"I'm taking seventeen high school juniors to Barstow," I replied simply, as if it was an everyday, normal occurrence, "In fact, I'm taking them *beyond* Barstow."

"Are you bringing any back?" was the retort as she slid away, hoping that what ever horrible mental aberration I had wasn't contagious.

In real life, I teach high school United States History, and we had just gotten to the 1920s. We are about to hit the Thirties and the Great Depression. As the Dust Bowl and the westward migration of those unfortunates usually referred to derisively as "Okies" are an important part of our history, and as the characterization of Route 66 as the "Mother Road" in the *Grapes of Wrath* is from this time, I thought that a field trip to really see what it was like was in order. At this point, I'm betting most of you agree that Tina's assessment of my mental health was sadly correct.

In many ways, I have to agree with her, but one doesn't survive thirty years as a high school teacher without a large dose of lunacy. Taking kids today on a Road Trip is indeed a daunting task. Taking a van load of kids who are not your own is positively Herculean! It is also important to expose kids to more than cell phones, iPods, and twitter. To connect them with our shared past. A Road Trip that gets off the ubiquitous interstate and lets them see what travel was like "back in the day" does this.

So, how does one go about this?

As a teacher, I have to admit to a few advantages. I can give an assignment to make sure they pay attention. In this case, a creative writing exercise. They would create letters home as if they were refugees from the Dust Bowl, telling the folks back home of the experience. They would be graded on creativity as well as accuracy and use of what they saw and learned along the way. In addition, I can spend class time setting up the trip, giving them background information. I also have wonderful colleagues who can team up with me. In this case, English teachers who showed clips of the movie version of *Grapes of Wrath* and had them read excerpts. You can also set ground rules for the trip.

So, having set up the trip, we loaded up the school van at 9:00 am. Another teacher would drive in her car as the van seated 15 and we had a total of 19 people, including chaperones. We left the school in North Hollywood and naturally got separated at the stop light just before the on ramp to the 170 freeway. At least with cell phones we could keep in touch. We finally hooked up in Victorville! This brings up a sticking point for such a trip. What to do with all the electronic appendages that have sprouted from teenagers in the last few years making them appear more like the Borg than humanoids? I set it up this way. To better compare today with ancient times (a.k.a. any time before they were born) they were allowed to use whatever electronic devices they wanted on the way out. At the turn around point, they would enter the Electronics Free Zone. Any use of cell phones and such would result in confiscation for the rest of the year!

So, off we sped, droning off the miles of interstate, kids busily texting and chatting, all of their attention focused inside the van. Up Cajon Pass and past the Summit Inn which I dually pointed out. Through

Hesperia, then Victorville, very little changing in the landscape. Rows of strip malls and fast food joints. The dull homogenization of America. After Victorville, things open up and the desert asserts itself. Long expanses of grey-brown desert under a wintery sky. By this time, the inevitably plaintive cries of "How much further?" and "Are we there yet?" followed by the equally inevitable "About 36 more hours" from the diver's seat, followed by the expected incredulous look. "*Mr. McCarthy...*" We were of course only about 36 *minutes* from Barstow and just a bit further to the turn around.

Down the hill to Barstow, right onto I-40, back into the desert and the kids are beginning to wake up and look out, puzzled at the houses that dot the landscape. "Who *lives* out here? What do they *do?*"

Finally, at the first off ramp for Newberry Springs we exited the interstate, just where Route 66 crosses on its meanderings eastward. There are two gas stations there. A nice looking Chevron and a dumpy, dirty place of questionable provenance. Guess which one I picked?

The Dagget Garage was a welcome sight. It meant travelers were nearing Barstow.
photo by the author

"All Out! All Out! We're here."

"Where?"

"Route 66, the Mother Road, this is it."

"What? The street?"

"Yeah, take a look, this is what we came for. Take a good look and we'll go home."

"*MR. MCCARTHY!!!...*"

"Can we use the rest room?"

"Are you kidding?"

"Can we use the rest room? *PLEASE??*"

"We drove two and a half hours to look at a road?"

"*CAN WE USE THE REST ROOM???*"

Did I mention that I teach in a school that has separate divisions for girls and boys? This year it was the girls' school's turn. At least this year I stopped at a gas station. The previous year, I took the boys' school and they peed in the desert. Some weren't so good at the "Don't Pee Into The Wind" thing. I worry about the future of mankind some days.

With that duty done, I gathered them around and declared the Electronic Free Zone and talked about coming in from Needles across the desert, the volcanic geology of the area

"Those mounds of black rocks are cinder cones, sort of like zits on the Earth's crust" (anything about zits gets teenagers' immediate and sympathetic attention) and that we would follow the road to Dagget, then Barstow.

Road Trippin'

As we turned off the highway in Barstow, I had them do some Urban Archeology. The part of Barstow that most people see today is in the wye created by the the I-15 and I-40. All the same fast food places as every other off ramp. As we climbed the hill into Old Barstow, I pointed out the older motels.

"These were the mainstay of Barstow in the 50s. This was a place many stopped before they got to LA, not wanting to push on in the dark. Dust Bowl migrants would of course have simply camped out. "

We next cruised past the dying center of Barstow. Rows of empty store fronts, dashed hopes of luring people further off the interstate than they would ever be willing to go. Turning right to cross the rail yard towards the station, the Harvey House and the Route 66 Museum, I pointed out the El Rancho Motel made entirely out of railroad ties.

At the Museum, we were met by Deborah Hodkin, the curator. She had very kindly opened the museum and had arranged for several old timers to be there to talk to the kids. I can't thank her and these volunteers enough. They were terrific! The girls looked around in wonder at all the Stuff. The Model T Phaeton in particular caught their attention.

"People *drove* that along the roads?" The hardiness of early travelers impressed them mightily!

After poking around the museum we went outside to tour the Harvey House. One of the old guys, tagged along just to make sure I didn't make any mistakes or leave anything out. We then ate lunch and headed back on the road.

"Are we going back now? Is that it?"

"Well, sort of. We're now hitting the old road."

And we did. After the outskirts of Barstow and Lenwood, we were in the open country and the two lane road that was what a main road was back then. Past abandoned gas stations and the remains of motor courts, derelict houses with collapsed roofs, desolation, and broken dreams, newer homes, and newer hopes. Past Helendale and Oro Grande, into Victorville, back on to the dreaded interstate and out of the time warp.

The next day in class was the payoff. Another group of budding young road trippers.

"Mr. McCarthy, that was sooo coool!"

"The people in the museum were REALLY nice. They really LOVE living out there!"

"That road was LONG! Imagine driving on that for DAYS?"

"I want to go back, that was SOOOO COOL!"

The author's US History Class, chowing down at El Deserito
photo by the author

91

US HighWay 395

--dateline Olympia, Washington

Yes folks, due to the miracles of modern technology, your faithful correspondent wrote this from the road! Wow, pretty cool, eh? Marianne and I decided to use my two week break to drive up to see my folks. Naturally, we couldn't do this the "normal" way (meaning I-yucky-5), we decided to take one of California's three "Mother Roads." Mother Road? Doesn't that mean Route 66? Well, no, not always.

Ya see, the Golden State is geographically a north/south state. Route 66 may be how many of you got here, and how most of you visited relatives back east, but us natives have spent our lives traveling north and south. That means our three main roads are north/south. The original California highway is the El Camino Real. The Mission Trail, founded by Fr. Juanipero Serra and his fellow Franciscans. Finally paved and dubbed by the US gummint "Highway 101." The second of course, the main street of California's agricultural empire is Route 99. If you check *Grapes of Wrath*, most of the action takes place *after* the Joads get to California and travel up and down 99, looking for work in the fields and orchards. The last of the three is the eastern most, the desert highway, the route to the eastern Sierra Nevada Mountains: US 395. This was to be our route north.

Most in SoCal know 395 as the way to Mammoth for skiing, but 395 is more, much more. It is the gateway to Mount Whitney. It is the gateway to Death Valley. The yin and yang of the continental United States. It is the route of the water we use to make SoCal possible. It is also the route of one of the darker chapters of our history. The route to Manzanar. What most people don't know is what is beyond Mammoth.

I think I can dispense with the usual route instructions. If you can't find US 395, you probably shouldn't be reading this. I want to focus more on what is there, and why this is such an excellent trip. You can divide 395 into three parts. The southern section is through the desert. You drive on the rim of Death Valley to the east and the Sierra Nevada's to the west. These magnificent mountains are most impressive from the eastern side. While the western slopes are tree covered forests, the eastern crags are almost lunar in their barrenness. Mt. Whitney and her sisters are jagged teeth, taking a bite out of a stark desert sky. The towns reflect this desert heritage. Olancha, Dunmovin, Cartago, Manzanar are desolate wide spots in the road. Sad remnants of motels and gas stations dot the road, testaments to travel in a different age, back when every car had a canvas Desert Cooler bag hanging from the hood ornament, back before air conditioning so all the windows were open despite the dust. The few extant motels seem to cater to travelers who are just too tired to drive further. There is little other reason to stop the night there.

The middle section is a quaint reminder of the outdoor recreation available in the Sierras: Independence, Lone Pine, Big Pine, Bishop. These are the gateway towns to the best trout fishing in the world. Since Bishop is an easy tank of gas from LA, it's the obvious place to gas up. If you have time, check out the railroad museum at Laws, just off 395. Great old narrow gauge stuff from when the Slim Princess plied the 3' rails down to Inyokern. One of my favorite sights in these towns are the neon signs on the sporting goods stores. There is no doubt that fishing is *the* outdoor sport. Not with that giant lighted trout jumping out into traffic! I remember being impressed by them when, as a Boy Scout, we'd make our annual trek to

Kennedy Meadows. Is there anything better than trout out of the stream straight into a hot buttered cast iron skillet? This section continues past the Mammoth turnoff, past Lee Vining and the road up Tioga Pass, Mono Lake, and Crowley Lake. Really pretty mountain scenery. You might want to take the side trip to Bodie, an honest to God real live ghost town.

We had left home early enough to get to Walker around lunch time and ran across a really neat place. The Mountain View BBQ. Run by Texas transplant Jeff Hinds, this place has some *fine* Que. Texas Style. Jeff and his ate brother built the place, including the intricate inlay work on the bar top. The smoker is out by the roadside and guarantees that this is the real deal. The Walker River descends to Carson City and Reno, "Biggest Little City in the World." Take the side trip to Virginia City. It's tacky and touristy and thoroughly enjoyable. Nevadans definitely have a different take on life! In Reno, check out what is now the National Automobile Museum (aka, what is left of Bill Harrah's massive collection). Its worth it just to see the Thomas Flyer that won the inaugural (and only) New York/Paris race. The damn *trophy* is worth the price of admission. Other than that, you can skirt Reno, but tank up. Things are going to get lonely. *Real Lonely*!

The third section is the weirdest. This part is high meadow land. Scrubby brush and wide open vistas. Long straights and sweeping bends of two lane blacktop and hardly a car in sight. The road climbs towards the Oregon border, getting twisty here and there to keep you honest.

The Mountain View BBQ, Near Walker, Ca
Photo by the author

We finally, as night was falling checked into the Frontier Motel in Alturas. About 12 hours of driving and 14 hours on the road. We were weary travelers. If you want to take a more leisurely pace, stop in Carson City then Burns, Oregon. We were out to make time. Alturas is an odd town. Not even sure why there is a town there. Ranching seems to be the way of life. The Frontier Motel is a classic. A sadly tired classic. At $40 for the night, it was decidedly better than the $100/night Best Western down the road. It's a family run place in need of business. The people were very friendly and the place was at least clean. Just tired. The real find was next door, what seemed like the only open eatery in Alturas on a Sunday night. Nipa's Thai/California Cuisine! Yeah, Thai food in the back of beyond! Good Thai food too! Marianne had the pad thai and I had the honey duck. Tasty, a bit spicy, proper jasmine rice. Erin, our server was helpful and really sweet, giving us tips on what was the good stuff.

Day two began at the obligatory O'Dark-Thirty. We had another 12 hours of driving to Olympia. This got to be an adventure. After gassing up (the place was actually closed but the pumps were turned on and took plastic) we headed into the dark morning towards Oregon and breakfast. Man, am I glad the Mustang has great headlights! As dawn broke somewhere north of Goose Lake the landscape was positively lunar. I'm talking seriously desolate. I mean *nothing* for miles and miles but miles and miles! Wide open straights and sweepers just made for some high speed motoring. We *averaged* some 75 mph all the way to Burns.

Hines and Burns are nice little towns, the Apple Peddler has a really good breakfast. Get this, a Belgian waffle topped with apple pie filling and whipped cream. UmmGood! A funky place to stay, if you are doing the three day version, is the Knotty Pine Motel. *Tiny* little place but friendly and family run.

The run from Burns to Pendleton is an odd mix. Eastern Oregon is divided by a series of east/west ridges, so 395 has long open straight stretches of semi-arid country then steep mountain passes and gorges with pine forests. This repeats about 5 times. It certainly keeps you on your toes. Pendleton is the home of the famous woolen mills. Visit and take the tour. Downtown Pendleton is a combination of old and new. One of the oldest western wear stores in the country, Hamley's has some amazingly fancy cowboy duds. Around the corner is a more modest Curio Shop (that's the name of the place) with lots and lots of turquoise. Yeah, Marianne heaven. We tried to get lunch there at the Corner Bistro. What a snotty place! All I wanted was a sub sandwich without mayo. "We don't make changes" was the reply. "But I'm allergic!" "We don't' make changes." We walked out. So, avoid this trumped up yuppie eatery.

The Trusty Steed outside of the Pendleton Woolen Mills
photo by the author

After this debacle, we just wanted out of Oregon. We headed to I-84 west to the Columbia Gorge. This is a spectacular drive. We've done it before, so we tried something else. North on I-82 to Yakima and west on US 12 to I-5. Whew, this did not go too well. Neat road, but a couple of idiot truckers who would speed up as you tried to pass them, the freaking FOREST FIRE we had to drive through, several single lane construction zones, and finally, the typical PacNW rain turned what should have been a wonderful last leg to Olympia into a real trial.

So, is 395 worth it? Absolutely! There is an amazing array of scenery. The people were nice (mostly) and rather amazed that we would drive 395 all the way. We got talking to a guy at a rest stop driving his hot rodded '55 Chevy panel truck down to the Bay Area for business. He loved this road and always took it whenever possible. Most of this trip is good old two lane blacktop, just like the good old days. Small towns that the highway does not avoid break up the journey and give it life and variety unobtainable on the dreaded interstate. 395 is a look at how we used to travel...395 is a journey into the past.

The King's Highway--101

"Show me the way to go home/I'm tired and I want to go to bed…" It was time to leave the soggy (well, let's be fair, it only rained one day while were up there in October no less!) Pacific Northwest. A good time was had by all, the parental and sibling units were glad we came and sorry to see us go. Naturally, we were *not* headed down the mother of all boring drives, I-5. Now I do have to be fair here to that much maligned highway. The trip through Washington isn't too bad really. Oregon is BOOOORING, but NoCal around Mt. Shasta is pretty cool. Dunsmuir is one of our favorite towns. Great railroad watching, great fishing, and good eats. Stay at the Cave Springs Motel if you visit. This is a classic with regular motel rooms and old style cabins-with-kitchenette to cook up that trout you caught earlier in the day. Still, that was not for us. Nope, the *real* California Mother Road beckoned. Highway 101. The El Camino Real. The King's Highway. The *first* west coast highway.

This was the route of the Franciscan padres, out to convert the locals and provide rest stops a day's journey apart. Imagine, a time when it took a day to get from San Gabriel to San Fernando. Modern times are *soooo* much better. In on the 10, up the 5 and…well, maybe not much of an improvement after all. Now the good fathers didn't go much beyond Frisco, but the trappers, traders and later the loggers did. And the Russians. Who? Yeah, durn Rooskies in the USA! Well, be nice, it was before Vlad Ulanov made a mess of the place. Remember, we bought Alaska from the Russians and their traders had established outposts as far south as Fort Ross, *south of* Ft. Bragg.

Although 101 is mostly four lanes, it still has a lot of the character of an old school highway. It's not all freeway, there are plenty of stretches where there is cross traffic. It still goes through small towns with local cafes and tourist "traps." In Washington and Oregon, it's all small town America. All about fishing and lumber and tourists. From I-5 in Washington, head west on WA-6, then south on 101. This will take you to Astoria, OR, and the mouth of the Columbia River. This was the end of the journey for Lewis and Clark on their assignment to see just how much land Tom Jefferson snookered Napoleon Bonaparte out of in the early 1800s.

Cross the magnificent (if a bit scary) Astoria Bridge and keep headed south. Obviously, the only directions for this trip are to head south on 101. Directions even a NASCAR Driver could follow (NASCAR GPS: "Turn left in ½ mile. Turn left in ½ mile. Turn left in ½ mile…). This section of coast is an easy rival for CA-1. That's a real concession for me, given how much grief I've heaped on Oregon over the years. Seriously, this is great stuff. Cool towns as well. Nehalem, Garibaldi, Tillamook, Newport, Waldport, and Coos Bay. Don't forget to stop at the Sea Lion Caves. Great little places, and all connected by this fantastic road!

By the time you hit California, you will be in need of a rest. Crescent City is a wonderful place. We like the Super 8 Motel. Family owned and one of the oldest motels in town. Dates back to 1964 or so. Of course, the whole *town* dates back to '64 after a tsunami did a job on the place. Right across the street is Meaghan's (daughter #2) favorite restaurant, the Fisherman's Restaurant. This place is great. All the locals seem to eat there, so there's always a lot of friendly chit chat. The Clam Chowder is some of the best I've ever had. The other seafood dishes are equally fine.

Next morning, continue south and either have breakfast in Eureka, or get going a bit later so you can stop in one of the all time great tourist spots: TREES OF MYSTERY! Sadly, one of the cool bits of funkiness that ToM was *famous* for is lost because of modern technology. Ya see, for decades, ToM wired a bumper sticker to the FRONT bumper of every car that stopped. For *miles*, no matter if you were headed north or south, you'd see "TREES OF MYSTERY" in bright red on a yellow placard. Great advertising ploy. Who could resist the lure when every other car had one? Can't wire stuff to modern bumpers, so no more blazing mobile proclamations enticing travelers to experience a True Mystery. I won't ruin the surprise about how mysterious these trees are. Just stop and enjoy. There is also Confusion Hill and Legend of Bigfoot to stop at along the way. Then there is the Avenue of the Giants. *TAKE THIS SIDE ROAD! DO NOT MISS THIS*, especially if you are in an open car or on a motorcycle. *Nothing* will put you more in awe of Nature. These redwoods are spectacular. While you're at it, make sure to drive through the Drive Through Tree.

Fisherman's Restaurant, Crescent City, CA
photo by the author

A good place to stop for lunch is Willits. This is the home of the famous Skunk Train that ran out to Ft. Bragg for years. It seems to go in and out of closure so I'm not sure if you can ride the Skunk any longer. Sad if ya can't. Where you stop for the night really depends on how much lollygagging you've been doing. Obviously, Frisco has a lot going for it. Monterey is extemly nice, although Cannery Row would make Steinbeck weep. Its SO Touristy/ Yuppie. There *is* some good food to be had though. South from Frisco isn't much fun, mostly an urban commute road, but GIlroy is cool. Roll down the windows for Gilroy and smell the GARLIC! Also some decent motels and eateries. Stop in one of the roadside shops that sells garlic stuff. AHHHHH! further south is King City and the Keiffer Inn. This place is a bit funky but kinda cool, the bad part of King City is that Denny's or Maggies (a Denny's with pretensions) is about the best you can get for food. DO NOT STOP AT THE MOTEL 6 in Salinas! This has to be the worst one we've ever been in. Vibra-massage via an out of balance dryer in the laundry room, mysterious reddish stains on the bed spread. EWWW! Even the In-n-Out across the street messed up our orders.

From here on down is the classic El Camino Real. Stop in at some of the missions. Each is unique and has a story to tell. Stop at Soledad Mission for a real sad tale. San Juan Bautista, San Miguel, San Luis Obispo, these are key names in California history. Check out the Madonna Inn in San Luis Obispo, for massively over the top interior design. There is also equally classic 101 scenery from here on down. Rolling hills dotted with oak trees. In the spring, the hills look like green velvet stained with poppies and mustard. In the summer, the soft round brown contours look like the beach covered with sunbathing beauties.

Wherever you stop for the night, make sure to time your trip so you can eat lunch at Jocko's in Nipomo. Best damn steak you have *ever* had. Period. From here, the route gets familiar. The beach cities of

Pismo, Oceano, Santa Barbara, Carpinteria, and Ventura are home stomping grounds for most of us. Spend some time in them. Too often we just drive by these days. They all offer great places to eat and stay.

When I wrote up the results of our Best Roads Survey, 101 was the clear winner and for good reason. The scenery is amazingly diverse, the food is wonderful and the road itself is one fine drive. Rediscover it if you haven't driven it lately.

The resurrection of the Blue Meanie--the author and Doc
Jones prepare for the maiden voyage
photo by Marianne McCarthy

Afterword

Ok, is this it? Are these *the* drives? Of course not. There are miles and miles of back roads out there, begging for people like us to scrub off some tire rubber on them. Lonely roads in need of company. Explore. Look about as you drive and really *see* things. Above all, as the late, great Chuck Johnson, our dispatcher at Embree Buses used to say, "Keep the shiny side up and the greasy side down."

And by the way, if you are interested, we sell many of the photos from this book along with a whole lot more through our website: www.mccarthypix.com. Stop by and check them out.

Appendix 1-Motels

Alturas, CA
Frontier Motel *
1033 North Main St.
530-233-3383
Funky, yet clean and quiet

Atascadero, CA
Motel 6 **
9400 El Camino Real
805-466-6701
Standard motel, clean

Beatty, NV *
Phoeniz/Atomic Inn
350 1st Street
775-553-2250
Funky, friendly, clean

Burns, OR
Knotty Pine Motel *
South West Circle Drive
541-573-7440
Funky, friendly, clean, tiny

Carson City, NV
Super 8 Motel *
2829 South Carson St.
775-883-7880
Clean but a bit noisy

Chama, NM
Chama Trails Inn *****
2362 S. State Highway 17
575-756-2156
Very Nice!, Clean, quiet

Crescent City, CA
Super 8 Motel **
685 Highway 101
707-464-4111
Clean, bit noisy-seals!

Dunsmuir, CA
Cave Springs *****
4727 Dunsmuir Avenue
(530) 235-2721
GREAT PLACE!

Gallup, NM
El Rancho Hotel *****
1000 E. US 66
800-543-6351
Historic! GREAT PLACE!

Guadelupe, CA
Far Western Tavern***
899 Guadalupe Street
(805) 343-2211
Steaks, diner food

Jackson, CA
Best Western Motel ***
200 N. State Highway 49
209-223-0211
Clean, Friendly

King City, CA
Keefer's Inn *
615 Canal St.
800-276-7415
Funky, clean

Martinez, CA
Super 8 Motel **
4015 Alhambra Ave.
925-372-5500
Clean and nice

Paso Robles, CA
Adelaide Inn ***
1215 Ysabel St.
805-238-2770
Very Nice

Paso Robles, CA
Best Western Black Oak Inn***
1135 24th St.
805-238-4740
Clean, friendly

Paso Robles
Motel 6 **
1134 Black Oak Dr
805-238-9090
Clean, standard motel

Porterville, CA
Holiday Inn Express ****
840 S. Jaye St.
559-782-1200
Friendly, very nice

St. Helena, CA
El Bonita Motel *****
195 Main St.
707-963-3216
Funky, but very nice!

San Simeon, CA
Motel 6 **
9070 Castillo Dr.
805-927-8691
Clean, standard motel

Seligman, AZ
Deluxe Inn Motel **
203 Chino St.
928-422-3244
Noisy-trains, clean, friendly, funky

William, AZ
9 Arizona Motel **
315 Historic US 66
928-635-4552
Funky, clean, friendly

William, AZ ***
Grand Canyon Railway Hotel
233 N. Grand Canyon Blvd.
928-635-4625
POSH!

Appendix 2-Restaurants

Alturas, CA
Nipa's ***
1001 N. Main St.
530-233-2520
Thai/California

Arcadia, CA
Denny's **
7 E. Huntington Dr.
626-446-3401
Standard diner, breakfast is best

Arroyo Grande, CA
Rusty Pig ***
564 Mesa View Dr.
805-489-3007
BBQ

Barstow, CA
Del Taco **
401 N. 1st Ave.
760-256-2810
Mexican fast food

Barstow, CA
Denny's **
1201 E. Main St.
760-256-0022
Standard diner, breakfast is best

Bishop, CA
Bar BQ Bill's-Oney's ***
187 S. Main St.
760-872-5535
BBQ

Cajon Pass, CA
Summit Inn Restaurant***
5970 Mariposa Road
Oak Hills, CA 92344-9002
(760) 949-8688
Diner food

Calistoga, Ca
Calistoga Inn *****
1250 Lincoln Ave.
707-942-4101
Upscale California cuisine

Calistoga, CA
Hydro Bar & Grill *****
1403 Lincoln Ave.
707-942-9777
Upscale grill

Carpinteria, Ca
The Palms ***
701 Linden Ave
805-684-3811
Steaks!

Carpinteria, CA
The Spot ***
389 Linden Ave.
805-684-3611
Burger Joint!

Carpinteria, CA
Tony's ***
699 Linden Ave.
805-684-3413
Italian/Pizza

Carpinteria, CA
Worker Bee Cafe **
973 Linden Ave.
805-745-1828
Diner food, breakfast is best

Centralia, WA
McMenamine's Olympic Club****
112 N. Tower Ave
360-736-1634
Upscale burgers/diner food

Chama, NM
High Country Restaurant*****
US 64
505-756-2384
Steaks/trout/mushroom soup!

Flagstaff, AZ
Mike & Rhonda's-
The Place***
21 S. Sitgreaves St.
928-774-7008
Diner food, good breakfast

Hines, OR
Apple Peddler***
540 U.S. 20
(541) 573-2820
Diner/waffles w/apple pie filling

Jackson, Ca
Teresa's Place *****
1235 Jackson Gate Rd.
209-223-1786
Family style Italian

Kingman, AZ
Mr. Dz ***
105 e. Andy Devine Ave.
928-718-0066
Diner food/burgers

Lacey, WA
Speedway Brewing Co*****
1225 Ruddell Rd SW
360-493-1616
BBQ!

Los Olivos, CA
Brothers' Restaurant at
Mattei's Tavern ****
2350 Railway Avenue
(805) 688-4820
Upscale California

Mariposa, CA
River Rock Inn & Deli Garden****
4993 7th St.
209-966-5793
Deli sandwiches

Nipomo, CA
Jocko's*************!
125 N. Thompson Ave.
805-929-3565
GREATEST STEAK EVER!

99

Appendix 2-Restaurants

Paso Robles, CA
Crooked Kilt *****
1122 Pine St.
805-238-7070
Pub Grub/fish&chips

Port Townsend, WA
Belmont Hotel *****
925 Water St.
360-385-3007
Seafood

Oceano, CA
Rock N Roll Diner ***
1300 Railroad St.
805-473-2040
Diner food/burgers

Ragged Point, CA
Ragged Point Inn ****
19019 Highway 1
805-927-5708
Upscale diner/great breakfast

San Juan Bautista, CA
Joan & Peter's
German Restaurant***
322 3rd St,
(831) 623-4521
German Deli

San Juan Bautista. CA
Restaurant ??
206 4th St,
(831) 623-4472
Basque Food. Duh!

Santa Barbara, CA
 (off Hwy154)
Cold Spring Tavern ***
5995 Stagecoach Road
(805) 967-0066
Upscale pub grub

Seligman, AZ
Road Kill Cafe/OK Saloon ***
502 W. Hwy 66
928-422-3554
Diner food, cute theme

Shandon, CA
Jack Ranch Cafe**
19215 E Highway 46
(805) 238-5652
Diner/James Dean Memorial

Shoshone, CA
Crowbar Cafe & Saloon ***
Highway 127
760-852-4123
Diner food

Tehachipi, CA
Village Grill **
410 East Tehachapi Boulevard,
661-822-112
Diner food

Walker (Coleville), CA
Mountain View Barbeque ****
106834 US 395
530-495-2107
BBQ-closed in winter

Williams, AZ
Cruiser's Cafe ***
233 Historic US 66
928-635-2445
Diner food

Williams, AZ
Max & Thelma's Restaurant**
231 N. Grand Canyon Blvd.
928-635-8970
American, buffet and menu

William, AZ
Rod's Steak House***
301 Historic US 66
928-635-2671
Steaks, DUH!

NOTE: *s were awarded based on how much we liked the place, how good the food was, how comfortable the room was, funk value, how good a time we were having, how many beers we drank, bribery, the usual stuff. This is HIGHLY subjective as we have odd tastes. If you don't agree, let me know, I'll mail you a dime to call someone who cares. This ain't the *Michelin Guide*, ya know.

Appendix 3-Must See Funky Stuff

Avenue of the Giants
http://avenueofthegiants.net/Zoom/map.htm

Bottle Forest
(Elmer Long's Bottle
Forest)
National Old Trails
Highway (Route 66)
between Helendale and
Oro Grande, CA

California Oil Museum
www.oilmuseum.net
1001 East Main Street
Santa Paula, CA 93060-2809
(805) 933-0076

Cameron Trading Post
www.camerontradingpost.com
54 Mouth North Hwy
Cameron, AZ 86020
(928) 679-2231

Confusion Hill Gravity House
www.confusionhill.com
75001 North Highway 101
Piercy, CA 95587-8805
(707) 925-6456

Cool Springs Museum/Gift Shop
http://www.coolspringsroute66.com/

Cumbres & Toltec Scenic RR
http://www.cumbrestoltec.com/

Drive Thru Tree Park
67402 Drive Thru Tree Road
P.O. Box 10
Leggett, CA 95585
Phone: 707-925-6363
E-mail: underwoodpark@aol.com

**Fort Humboldt State Historic Park
& Logging Museum**
3431 Fort Avenue
Eureka, CA 95503-3828
(707) 445-6567

Grand Canyon Caverns
www.gccaverns.com
Mile Marker 115
Route 66, Peach Springs, AZ 86434
(928) 422-3223

Grand Canyon RR
1 800-THE-TRAIN (843 8724)
www.thetrain.com

James Dean Memorial
Jack Ranch Cafe**
19215 E Highway 46
(805) 238-5652

Railtown 1897 State Historic Park
Fifth Avenue and Reservoir Road,
Jamestown,
California 95327
(209) 984-3953
www.railtown1897.org

Hornitos, CA
http://www.ghosttowns.com/states/ca/
hornitos.html

Legend of Big foot
2500 Highway 101
Garberville, CA 95542
(707) 247-3332

March Field Air Museum
22550 Van Buren Blvd
March Arb, CA 92518-2400

Mt. Rainier Scenic Railway
Mt. Rainier Scenic Railroad, PO Box 250,
Mineral, WA 98355
www.mrsr.com/

National Automobile Museum
10 Lake Street
Reno, NV 89501-1558
(775) 333-9300
www.automuseum.org

Orange Empire Railway Museum
2201 South A Street
Perris, CA 92570

Pendleton Woolen Mills
1307 SE Court Pl,
Pendleton Oregon 97801

Rainbow Rock Shop,
101 Navajo Boulevard,
Holbrook, Arizona.

Route 66 Museum, Barstow
681 N. First Avenue
Barstow, CA. 92311
760-255-1890
http://www.route66museum.org/

Scotty's Castle
123 Scottys Castle Road
Death Valley, CA 92328
(760) 786-2392

Trees of Mystery
15500 US Highway 101 North
Klamath, CA 95548-9351
(707) 482-2251
www.treesofmystery.net

Virginia City
www.virginiacity-nv.org/

Western American RR Museum/
Casa El Deserito
685 North First Street
Barstow, CA 92311
(760) 256-WARM

Winchester Cheese
32605 Holland Road
Winchester, CA 92596-9696
(951) 926-4239
www.winchestercheese.com

These are just some of the funky things to see that I've mentioned. I put in what contact information I could find. Most have websites so you can check them out before hand, find out hours, etc. There's plenty more out there, the best stuff is the stuff you just happen across. Rule One of Road Trips: Serendipity Rules!

AppeNdiX 4

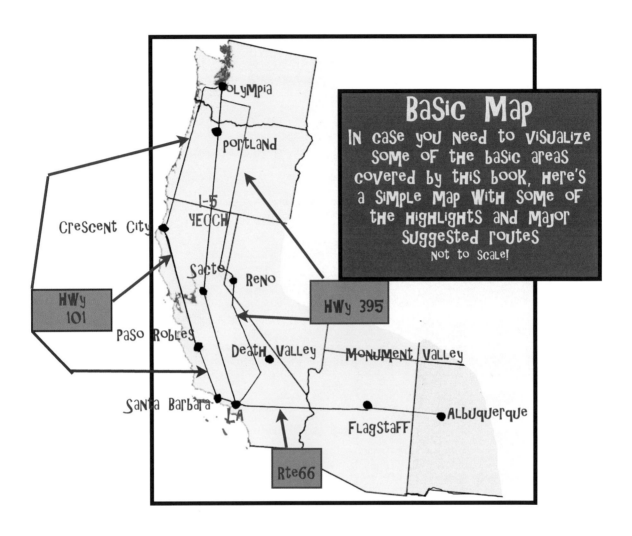

Olympia

portLaNd

I-5
YEOCH

CresceNt City

Sacto   ReNo

HWy
101

Paso RobLes

Death VaLLey   MoNumeNt VaLLey

Santa Barbara
LA   Albuquerque

FLagstaFF

HWy 395

Rte66

BaSic Map
IN case you Need to visuaLize
some of the basic areas
covered by this book, here's
a simpLe Map with some of
the HigHLigHts aNd Major
suggested routes
Not to scaLe!

Made in the USA
Charleston, SC
01 July 2010